Published in the United States of America by Shareve Communications, an *imprint of Southern Girls General Store, Inc.,* 1390 Columbia Ave., #215, Lancaster, PA 17603, USA

Printed in the United States of America

ISBN: 978-1-937587-03-1

Living Well: Black Women Interracial and Intercultural Marriage— Book 4

Black Women Marrying Multiculturally and Living Well: How the Average Black Women Can Marry at Her Level or Higher, Live Well, and Make Better Choices in the Global Village—Using a Proven, Common Sense Approach

—Essays and Conversations—

Eve Sharon Moore

▪ SHAREVE COMMUNICATIONS▪
Dover, Delaware

ABOUT THE AUTHOR

Eve Sharon "Evia" Moore was interviewed by the Associated Press over a period of weeks in 2007, and her website **BlackFemaleInterracialMarriage.com** was spotlighted in an Associated Press article about the surge in black women entering interracial marriages. This popular niche website encourages Black women to embrace the abundance in life, which includes taking advantage of all of their dating and mating options by inviting men of *all* races and cultures into their potential relationship pool.

Evia is an interracially-married essayist, interracial and intercultural relationship adviser, fiction writer, podcaster, and publisher of a growing series of books, newsletters, and podcasts on the subject of interracial and intercultural marriage

Visit: BlackFemaleInterracialMarriage.com

▪Make a donation at the site and receive the popular newsletter: ***VETTING MEN 101: The Secret Life of Plants*** (all 12 issues—with 3 of Evia's podcasts**).** This newsletter highlights many of the important criteria and issues that women should be aware of when evaluating men for serious relationships as well as much other pertinent information that relates to the "mating dance."

Acknowledgements

To my awesome sons: you always inspire me and are my greatest reward for living.

To my ultra-supportive mates who shared their wisdom and supported me in all of my endeavors: I would never have stepped out to write this book without your ever-present support.

To my wise father, shrewd mother, uncles, aunts, and visionary grandmother who instilled in me much common sense and taught me that black women deserve to be loved, cherished, and adored, that I must never accept less: your words marked my path.

Special thanks to my "chief" blog researcher and the legion of volunteer blog contributors who devoted themselves to providing me with fresh links to articles, pictures, videos, and commentary to compel black women in the United States and similar situations to exercise their numerous options in all realms of life, to embrace the abundance in life, and "live well."

The choice of a mate is the single most important decision that a woman makes in her life, especially if there are to be children. If she chooses her mate wisely, she and her children will reap many rewards. But if she chooses poorly, she has paved the way for herself and her offspring to suffer, for generations!

—Eve Sharon Moore

ALSO BY EVE SHARON MOORE

More interracial and intercultural relationship titles:

*Black Women: Interracial and Intercultural Marriage
Book 1—FIRST AND FOREMOST (Published 2009)*
**See Essay Topics in BOOK 1 on p. 231 of this book.

*CHOICES: Black Women Interracial and Intercultural
Marriage—Book 2 (Published 2009)*
**See Essay Topics in BOOK 2 on p. 231 of this book.

*RECIPROCITY: Black Women Interracial and
Intercultural Marriage—Book 3 (Published 2010)*
*See Essay Topics in BOOK 3 on p. 232 of this book.

~~UPCOMING Titles in the Series:

*VETTING: Black Women Interracial and Intercultural
Marriage—Book 5*

*BEAUTIFUL YOU: Black Women: Interracial and
Intercultural Marriage—Book 6*

*SELF-CARE: Black Women: Interracial and
Intercultural Marriage—Book 7*

*BROADEN: Black Women: Interracial and
Intercultural Marriage—Book 8*

*SEIZE YOUR POWER: Black Women: Interracial and
Intercultural Marriage—Book 9*

*SOAR: Black Women: Interracial and Intercultural
Marriage—Book 10*

(Published sequentially through June 2013)

Contents

INTRODUCTION

THE ORIGIN OF THIS BOOK

LIVING WELL: Black Women Interracial and Intercultural Marriage BOOK 4—is the fourth book in the ongoing series, compiling my commonsense essays and conversations with thousands of readers regarding the surge in black women—mainly upwardly mobile African-American in the United States—choosing to mingle romantically with and marry men from other races and cultures. This is also known as *out-marriage* and *exogamy*. Some people consider this turn of events revolutionary and *evolutionary* in the social sense for black women because the overwhelming majority of these non-black men who date and marry black women are white men.

In the past, virtually 100% of African-American women married only African-American men or black men. However, two conditions have drastically changed this pattern: (1) greatly lessened racial and social barriers between white men and upwardly mobile black women in the United States, and (2) a large percentage of African-American men do not seek marriage, or are either not available or not prepared for marriage, for a variety of reasons. Approximately only 35% of African-American men are married at this point. Twenty-two percent of them married non-black women in 2008. Among African-American women, 70% are presently unmarried.

When conditions in the environment change negatively, people with *common sense* who plan to survive and thrive also change their behavior to offset these unfavorable conditions. African-American women out-marrying men of other races and cultures is the normal or commonsense response, given these markedly altered social conditions.

I am an African-American woman, a writer, and a lifelong student of comparative cultures or *ethnology,* my undergrad major. My first marriage was to a born-and-bred West African man with whom I shared a multi-year marriage and many enlightening experiences regarding culture and race while living both in Africa and the United States with him. I'm now married to an American white man.

My series of books will serve the future as a record of much in the *hearts and minds* of black women currently as well as the views of a cross-section of others regarding the prevailing circumstances that surround black women out-marrying, in the first decades of this millennium. Capturing Black women's views as events unfold about the circumstances in their lives is of significant historical importance. Future readers will read exactly what black women were thinking during this time, and in their own words about various factors in their lives.

The series of essays in each book and the broad scope of the accompanying thousands of comments will thus help to fill a critical void. Historical accounts are usually devoid of black women's perspectives or only have a sparse representation.

Many black women, men of various races, and others are avid readers and viewers of my site. In the numerous notes I've received, they have hailed the value of both my commonsense perspectives as well as the views and experiences of many of the commenters. They love and learn from the conversations.

On the site, I share thoughts and a wide variety of experiences from my decades-long journal, recounting my life as an interculturally and interracially married woman. I often advise my readers to "take what you can use and toss the rest." I'm known on my website as "Evia."

As a strong proponent of quality relationships and marriages for African-American women, the gist of many of my essays urges black women in the United States, in particular, to broaden their dating and marriage scope to include *quality* men from the *entire global village*. I implore them to take a proactive stand on this issue of finding a suitable and compatible, quality mate of any race or ethnic background. The quality of the man is the most important factor. Black women must vet each suitor and look for evidence that he possesses the traits, abilities, desire, and drive to meet the challenges of performing well as a husband and a father. The world is now a global village. African-American women who seek marriage and children must rip themselves from their comfort zone, when necessary, and mingle fluidly in the world, but only with compatible men who possess the capabilities that indicate a high likelihood of strong performance as husbands and fathers.

A great proportion of African-American women seek to find a loving and lovable mate of quality, marry, and have children—in *that* order. Therefore, the central theme of my essays is to encourage African-American women to realize that they have many choices available towards reaching that goal.

I stress that black women must choose mates wisely. They must be radically proactive regarding mating only with quality, loving, lovable, suitable, and compatible men. The core purpose of my essays is to energize and *activate* African-American women towards that end. I urge them to reach out and embrace the many choices beyond their immediate environment for a fulfilling life, including love and marriage to a quality mate.

I define a quality man, in this regard, as one who is ready, willing, and capable emotionally, mentally, and financially of meeting the challenges of life as an adult male. Or, if he's a younger man, he must be in serious preparation to do so.

The essence of creating a quality life is another theme I've written much on in some of my essays. I compel African-American women to live an abundant life in all respects, or to "live well." For many women, a loving, committed mate is an important component in living a life of abundance.

In July 2006 when I began writing these hundreds of blog essays that make up my continuing series of what I consider now—"teaching" essays, I was a *newbie* blogger. I naively had no clue that anyone would be particularly interested in reading what I wrote about my marriage to a white man. My blog was my journal—not a private one, but a written account of some of my experiences as an interracially married woman. I had dated men of other nationalities and races, since I was eighteen. I majored in ethnology as an undergraduate in college, married a Nigerian man, and lived abroad with him. I wrote often about my intercultural relationships. The dynamics of intercultural and interracial relationships became the norm for me. Therefore, my decision to marry a white man was not an unusual move for me.

I soon discovered I had encountered a virtual 'live wire' by openly discussing a topic in my essays that many people consider *taboo*. My happy marriage to a white man was just more than many people could stomach. Although I received an overwhelming number of supportive notes in my private e-mailbox, it also became obvious that my essays irritated some, to the extent that they wished a monstrous caterpillar would swallow me.

Please note that African-Americans are the black reference group for my essays, although there may be similar concerns among other groups of blacks. Many black people in the United States still have great difficulty discussing the topic of black women and white men dating or black women entering loving, marital relationships with white men, or anything regarding interracial relationships of the black woman-white-skinned man type. A number of researchers have contacted me saying it's difficult to find material at all about the black woman-white man relationship, unless it's sexual or pornographic, despite the great increase in black woman-white man dating and marriages.

People are simply not talking or writing about it or only scantily. Many are apparently very reluctant to discuss this topic because of the ever-strained state of race relations in the United States, which is due to present-day racist structures stemming from the country's sordid history of chattel slavery perpetrated upon captured Africans by Europeans.

However, if there were courses on interracial dating, love, sex, and marriage between black women and white (European-American) men at the turn of the millennium in the United States, this series of essays and particularly the thousands of penetrating comments from a cross-section of readers would be required reading. In a nutshell, the comments from my readers are powerful. They literally changed my life.

All the essays and comments are plucked from my blog site: BLACK FEMALE INTERRACIAL MARRIAGE Ezine (located now at *www.blackfemaleinterracialmarriage.com*) which my readers have made enormously popular by visiting to the tune of millions of visits since July 2006 and reading millions of words of my writings, along with the numerous comments from readers. I thank them for spreading my name throughout the blogosphere and bringing many other readers to my site, many of whom have written me to say that my essays have uplifted them and spurred them to make life-altering changes.

From the very beginning, I was contacted for interviews by academicians, other bloggers, magazines, newspapers, radio and TV program producers, and in early 2007, I was contacted by a reporter from the Associated Press, who did a series of interviews with me for an article regarding black women in interracial relationships and marriages with white men. This culminated in an August 2007 Associated Press article about the subject, and my blog was spotlighted. The article was picked up by CNN online news, USA Today, ABC news and numerous major and minor news outlets worldwide and grabbed attention like a raging gasoline fire.

Within 36 hours of the article appearing, more than 10,000 visitors came to my site from all parts of the globe. I was thunderstruck that a topic as familiar to me as sliced bread could interest so many people!

Others often describe me as "courageous." I've never thought of myself as that. I am, however, a strong proponent of marriage for African-American women. I'm a believer in practical consequences and real effects, a pragmatist. Many among the 70% of black women in the United States are unmarried largely due to the unavailability of *quality* marriage mates in the pool of men they've been traditionally slated to marry—black American men. Therefore, it is merely logical for these women to broaden their dating and marriage pool to include *all* interested, suitable, and compatible men of quality in the global village. As you read the thousands of comments that accompany the whole series of essays, it becomes apparent that the vast majority of upwardly mobile African-American women commenters agree with this sheer commonsense remedy.

In the United States, the bulk of the non-black men are white American men. Whites comprise roughly 70% (2006 census) of the U.S. population, and blacks are 13%. Many African-American women share a familiar cultural background and values with those of many white American men.

In 2009, however, my commonsense position is largely considered radical and even heretical in segments of the black community in the United States, even though most blacks know that the pool of marriageable black men and those who are interested in marriage has shrunk to a thin stream. Seemingly, many black people would prefer that these black women remain unmarried. At the same time, black women in America are constantly criticized for having children out of wedlock—the "babymama" phenomenon.

The women obviously cannot marry unavailable or uninterested black men and they shouldn't marry unloving men, or those who are unequipped to meet the challenges of marriage and family life. However, no high profile black "leader," black politician, thought leader, or anyone of national visibility has addressed the issue of whom these millions of women are supposed to marry before having children. Despite that, even the mere suggestion that it would make good sense for black women to include white men in their pool of committed relationship candidates is met with anger, accusations of "disloyalty," "sellout," and sometimes-physical threats by black men, some of whom exclusively date and marry interracially themselves. Many black men express their approval of interracial dating and marriage—for black men only.

The volumes of fear and confusion expressed by the black women commenters regarding IR dating and marriage fascinated me. Their sentiments were unfamiliar to me, since I have always dated and married outside my group. Their feelings became a major incentive to continue writing the essays. Fearful of black community condemnation and ostracism, many so-called "strong" black women succumb to community and self-inflicted pressure to mate with the only "approved" man—a black man, at a time when there is a critical shortage of marriageable and marriage-interested American black men.

This often results in man sharing or serially mating with black men who have not equipped themselves to meet the emotional and financial responsibilities of a relationship with a woman or the demands of fatherhood. Numerous other black women simply wed themselves to the church or community and live a life of solitary confinement on the romantic front as they wait in quiet desperation for their "Mr. Right Black Man" to appear.

Although some people tend to view African-American women as *amazingly strong*, which is translated as something akin to a separate species of mythical Amazonian women, I want to emphasize that African-American women are the same as other women in the world. They dream of children and a stable home life with a responsible, supportive, loving partner at their side. Given that so few of them are able to readily attain this, many of them are frequently encouraged by other blacks in their environment to *wait* endlessly for their *black* 'knight' to appear.

In order to keep the women complacent while waiting, this ever-adapting message continues to contort itself to explain to the women why he hasn't appeared, yet. To remain hopeful and inside their comfort zone inside black community circles, many of the women cooperate in helping to delude other black women to remain patient and waiting too. A proportion of them put on a brave face each day and takes refuge in what I've labeled in this context as *magical thinking*.

Many non-African-Americans, including other black

ethnics, are not aware of this highly effective indoctrination process that maintains the status quo inside the African American community. Some of these others have asked me why it is that so many hard-working, seemingly intelligent black women limit themselves to African-American men as mates and focus, usually without help from the fathers, on raising the children and 'saving the black community,' yet receive merely minimal gratitude, if *any*, for their sacrifices and effort.

Despite the devastation it takes on their emotional and physical health along with their finances, the fact is that often many of the women themselves can't explain in any rational way why they do it. There actually is no logical reason to continue investing the bulk of assets (time, energy, money, life) in any entity that continues to deliver faint or often negative returns. Many African-American women continue on this course, however, and continue to end up struggling, poor, and alone.

As many of the comments clearly state or reveal, this is very harmful to the women and this is evident in the dismal health statistics of black women, many of whom "medicate" themselves in various ways. One way is with food, and they lead the nation in 2009 in weight-related illnesses: diabetes, cancer, heart problems, and a host of other debilitating maladies. Commenters continually make the point that the black community could not survive without 'riding on the backs' of black women, yet does not consider it important to make the basic needs of black women, a priority. Aside from lip service, there is nothing in the situation that even shows there is a functioning "community" involved. A community is a give-and-take place. There is a large degree of uplifting, mutual exchange, or *reciprocity* between people in a functioning community.

The conclusion from dozens of discussions and hundreds of comments: *reciprocity* is sorely lacking in the so-called black community, when it comes to meeting the basic needs of African-American women. Many of the black men, who had the resources to help, have fled physically, mentally, and emotionally. Therefore, from the standpoint of many blacks who remain in a black residential area and even those who inhabit mainly a "black" mental construct, but who may live outside of the physical black residential area, this deluding of black women will continue—in order for the women to maintain the illusion of the black "community." Many black women receive much subtle pressure to believe in and keep in place a safe harbor for everyone but themselves. Indoctrinated to put their own safety, security, and general betterment low on the list, many African-American women are strongly complicit in supporting an arrangement that does not meet their needs or those of other American black women.

Reciprocity is critical in any healthy or worthwhile relation-ship. High praise is often given to black women who give *selflessly* to the community, but most of the women have not learned to demand that others meet their needs, or give back to them.

Shortly after I began blogging, many black women came to my site to discuss their frustrations about being *boxed in* by the so-called black community. Woman after woman pointed out that the "community:" 1) provides no effective protection from the misogyny nor the general violence and sexual attacks from an assortment of community predators who physically and emotionally prey on women and their children, often with impunity, 2) presents severely low-quality or limited, nonexistent marital options, 3) often blames the women for the community's demise, 4)burdens them (like 'mules') alone with the task of "saving the community," 5) expects black women to successfully socialize and raise male children alone, a feat that is unparalleled in general human history, 6) pressures black women to prop up or carry severely dysfunctional or *damaged beyond repair* black males (dbrbm), 7) offers scant or no reciprocity to black women for the self-sacrifices made by them to keep the traditional black church and black community from disappearing altogether.

Much of the women's discontent also focuses on the un-abashed double standard—held by many American black men and some segments of black women—that gives tacit approval for black men to mingle with and marry non-black women while pressuring black women to remain "loyal" to black men only.

My blog became the site of a rallying cry from a wide cross-section of black women with the central message that black women must make use of their options to meet and marry mates from the entire global village just as black men increasingly do and just as white, Asian, Hispanic, and other women and men. Black women in America cannot mend or hold up the black community, *alone*. Instead, black men are needed to build, repair, and sustain the community with equal involvement and commitment. Without that, the American black community will continue to sink.

Some of my readers and I encouraged others to spread the

commonsense remedy that African-American and other black women in a similar predicament must exercise all of their options to mate and marry the highest quality, loving, and lovable man of any skin shade or background. Since the vast majority of the women feel that they lack a community that protects them and safeguards their interests, black women must make it a priority to promote and protect their own interests, 'first and foremost.' Each woman lifting herself will lift the entire community.

I urged readers to start their own blogs to help to get the word to millions of black women that no woman is alone in her yearnings for a loving partner and fulfillment as a woman. My essays and the poignant comments struck a chord with many black women in the United States and beyond who endure sexist oppression that compounds the racial oppression many black women face. They heard the word and responded.

Thus, my blog and similar ones that sprang up became "freedom" oases offering understanding, acceptance, support, encouragement, ideas, strategies, tactics, and practical advice for numerous black women who visited often to mingle with like-minded others. They, in essence, have formed the *community* they've been looking for. These women sought affirmation and guidance from a caring sisterhood as they strove to actualize their goal of finding loving and lovable, quality men for partners, and securing a relationship with fully committed men who possess fatherhood desires and the emotional and financial ability to be involved fathers in the lives of their children. Millions of black women in the U.S. desire marriage *before* having children, and want, in general, to exercise their options to 'live well.' These are normal desires of most women worldwide. African-American women are no different.

However, when typical African-American women express these desires, they do not often get the support of other blacks around them. Those around them frequently scold them for being impatient and "selfish." They are told to focus primarily on uplifting the black community, first. Others, who they trust, urge them to subscribe to the notion that their "Mr. Right" is on the way. Confused and lacking support, many black women give in to this social pressure. They neglect their own needs. They wait or they settle for an unsuitable male.

Through my essays and the comments section, many of the women began to realize that they must not limit themselves in any way. Marriage-oriented African-American women must not waste time with a focus on ANY man who is not interested in marriage.

One of my more controversial positions is my frequent urgings to black women to "marry well," by marrying a man who is at least as equally upwardly mobile and ambitious as the woman is. I explain, in meticulous detail, why any black woman of childbearing age has to be extremely particular in choosing the man she spends time with sexually, in order to avoid abortions, unplanned children, and blighted lives.

In 2009, single black women with children comprise the most impoverished demographic in the country. My mantra is: *the decision to be sexually intimate with any man is absolutely the most important single decision a black woman (or any woman) makes in her life since its impact may be felt for generations. Based on her choice, she—and any child who may come from this sexual intimacy—might either sink or soar.*

Detractors deliberately misinterpret me when I suggest to black women to include progressive-minded, enlightened white men and other non-black men in their dating and marriage pool. This is often distorted to mean that I am telling black women to embrace racist white men and reject *all* black men. This amounts to outright lies and gross twisting of my message, since I have never encouraged any association between black women and racist white men or the rejection of quality black men. These contrived distortions aim to discredit my message and cause fear.

Many black women readers shrewdly saw through these attempts to discredit me and my message. They stated in private notes to me and in their comments that the major underlying purpose of the critics' lies is—to keep as many black women as possible, confused and available as a "safety net" for favors and as sexual partners for black men to use as they wish. This is often why even black men who exclusively date or are married to non-black women, still don't want black women to date or marry white men.

A black male commenter pointed out that some African-American men also have the fear that as more black women date and marry non-black men and non-AA men, the desirability index of AA men as sexual and relationship partners will be reduced among all women. He said AA men reason that high demand for them pushes up their value in the mating market among *all* women.

The critical point that my essays and the comments focus on throughout this maze of emotions, perspectives, and politics is the lack of regard for black women's needs as individual women—the right of each black woman to 'live well.' What quickly becomes apparent is that the black woman's right to opportunities for love and happiness is rarely seen as a priority by anyone, not even by the women themselves.

Both the positive and negative responses to my blog became so overwhelmingly intense at times that I had to take breaks from it frequently. Being on the forefront of what some have called a "black women's empowerment" movement (though I consider it to be the *common sense imperative*) is emotionally draining. Many people feel they have the right to dictate to an American black woman how she should think, how she should live her life, who she should love or shouldn't love, or whether she should even be loved. I frequently remind black women that the Constitution of the United States grants every adult the *right* to choose the person of their choice to love and marry, irrespective of race, culture, religion, etc.

My essays compel black women to look out for their interests 'first and foremost' (subtitle of my BOOK 1) and without apology. This is common sense because 'self-preservation is the first law of nature.' Black women must position themselves to, not only survive, but also *thrive*. They will succeed at doing this only if they make it a rule to promote and protect their interests and require reciprocity from others.

The primary lesson that I want women readers to draw from my blog's teaching essays regarding love and marriage is that a "good lovin" man can be from any compatible background, and of any skin shade or race. African-American women of marriageable age should focus on marriage to a *quality* man as the goal, especially if the woman plans to have children. Though marriage is not a perfect institution, it's the best arrangement that humans have devised for having and rearing children and for meeting myriad other needs of women and men.

A family starts with marriage—a legal commitment or one that is sanctioned by a particular culture or society. It is the basic building block of any community or nation. When the *majority* in any community consists of non-committed men and women engaging in recreational, no-strings-attached sex with each other, the result will always be social chaos, as we currently see in many black residential areas. For this reason, there won't be any significant improvement in the American black community until a large percentage of the residents begin choosing mates properly, and marrying with the focus on a family *bond*. There is no way around this.

This is why I stress that black women in the West who seek quality mates for marriage must broaden their selection pool by including men from *all* backgrounds because as I frequently point out, "there are many more men of quality in the ocean than in a backyard puddle." It is the common sense imperative for American black women, in particular, to embrace the wide variety of men in the global village who appreciate their beauty and worth, men who regard them as desirable mates for marriage, and to become indifferent towards *any* man who views them otherwise.

American black women who desire marriage must promote the message that they desire marriage, but only with men who are equipped for, or (depending on age) can show evidence that they are equipping themselves for marriage (emotionally and financially). It is foolish for a black woman who wants to marry to spend time with *any* man who does not meet these simple criteria.

It would seem unnecessary, but I want to emphasize to upwardly mobile American black women that there is no shortage of quality men in the global village. They simply must enlarge their selection pool. There are numerous black ethnic men (intercultural option), white men, white-skinned men (interracial option), and other men in America and throughout the world who are very much attracted to black women's beauty, sense of purpose, and being. I hear from many of these men. Yet, too often, both sides tend to focus excessively on race and other minor, surface details.

My husband and I both realize that "race" is simply a social construction, created and kept alive by immoral, self-centered, human beings who have exploited the worst in human nature to keep a lot of "white" and "black" people stuck inside the race construct, while selected others reap the benefits and privileges. My husband's skin shade is lighter than mine is, and my hair, with its much tighter coil, differs from his by the degree of the coil. All the rest is simply a part of the "race" fairy tale or nightmare.

There is no essential difference between "races" of human beings. Progressive-minded, thriving-oriented people realize they are being manipulated and do not cooperate with the construction of race.

[NOTE 1: *www.blackfemaleinterracialmarriage.com* is the Ezine companion to this book. Most pictures cited in this book plus numerous other photos of famous and ordinary interracial/intercultural couples comprised of black women and their non-black or other-culture spouses or significant others can be viewed in picture galleries at the Ezine or accessed there. While at the site, please browse through the sections containing a wide array of videos, articles, links, and podcasts related to this topic.

NOTE 2: Most of the teaching essays and the accompanying comments are or will be available for purchase in various formats: paperback, audio, and for a variety of e-reading devices.

NOTE 3: Most of the essays in this book are out of the sequence in which they were written. The comments from readers are presented—*as received*, except for editing of gross misspellings, typos, and grammar styles that would interfere with reader comprehension. (Some commenters are non-Americans, which is reflected in the spellings of certain words.) All comments were supplied voluntarily and with the knowledge they would be published.

Abbreviations, colloquialisms, and vernacular expressions are explained in the *Glossary*. I welcome your comments, questions, suggestions, and helpful corrections. Please share them with me at: eviamoore@gmail.com]

1

Living Well: Critical Thinking Can Set You Free!

August 11, 2008

I was incredibly busy this weekend. Along with setting up 2 new blogs: the *Romance* blog and my *In Other Words* (focus on critical thinking) blog, I gave my husband Darren a fun-fested, food-filled birthday party on Saturday that I'd been planning for weeks. He was so excited—though he was real *cool* about it. ☺

The weather was idyllic, the menu—made from many garden goodies—was delicious, and the guests ate, drank, and laughed long into the night. Thanks go out to all of the family and friends who helped or contributed because things got really hectic in the last hour before the party started!

Big thanks to two of my sister-in-laws and two girlfriends who were boiling the sweet corn and potatoes and checking on the details of things inside and outside and also to my relatives who came to help out.

Also, I don't want to leave out my thanks to the 2 brother-in-laws who went to get the cake. And *big-time* thanks to the brother-in-law who did the grilling! I hope I'm not leaving anyone out. I know some of the family members read my blog. I appreciate *all* that you did! And last, but not least, I so appreciate every single family member and guest who came from far and near, without whom there could have been no party. ☺ Whew!

Anyway, I'm posting the comment below from a troll because it presents me with a *teachable moment*. Yes, it's obviously from a troll beating the *'give da po' bm a chance'* drum. I find it amazing that DBRbm and their sympathizers keep reading and commenting here. They know that most likely their comment will be rejected. I've deleted dozens of their comments in the last 2 weeks, yet many of them still write me. This is how I *know* they want me to hear them. I find this surreal. Why pester *me*? I'm just *one* interracially married black woman. Do they pester interracially married black men?

Yet they *claim* they don't want me or my commenters to talk about them here. Hmmmmmm? ☺ They apparently don't think I'm intelligent enough to see through this bogus claim. But I would never be able to create such a perfect teachable moment as this troll's comment has presented, so I thank him or her for this gem.

How do dim-witted people who operate like this survive these days? Let me just say, that people who operate on this low-thinking level may survive, but are not going to *thrive* in the world we live in, where there are many very shrewd competitors pursuing scarce resources. There are some very brainy people of all backgrounds, races, and ethnicities out there who can connect a lot of the dots. But these trolls and similar foolish others are obviously used to peddling all kinds of low-level tripe to bw and to the bc, and getting over.

The fact is that as more bw learn that they have choices and learn how to take advantage of those choices, there will be a mass exodus of these black women away from lower caliber men. The period we're in now is a period in which many AA women are trying to learn the steps they need to use to both access and take advantage of all their options. This period will henceforth be known as "the quiet before the stampede."

Have y'all noticed how often DBRbm men (and their sympathizers) get away with saying practically anything, no matter how insane around AAs and no one will call them out on it because no one wants to hurt the feelings of AA men. However, most AA females are not allowed to get away with saying stupid stuff. We know before we say it, that we will have to explain or defend anything we say. Therefore, that makes us mentally sharper.

Some of you non-AA readers may know by now that all kinds of blame and responsibility are heaped on black girls and bw for even the slightest things, but you may not know that AA females tend to be sliced and diced for saying or doing stupid stuff. People cannot wait to pounce on us. LOL !

AA females are held *responsible* and *accountable* and this is why most of us *know* beyond any doubt that we have to either achieve or get ready to live a mangy dog's life—with not much in between. Very few people in this society are going to *accept* any kind of sad sob story from an AA female. That was one of the first lessons I learned as a girl.

Anyway, here's the comment. (It was so poorly written until I had to correct *some* major grammatical errors to make it readable.) It shows clearly how so often, bm of this type (and their sympathizers/defenders) tend to think they can get away with saying anything, no matter how ludicrous:

> *I am a bm. Two years ago, I lived in a furnished room. I maked 9.70 an hour and I had (and still own and run) my own repair business on the side. I got married last year to a woman who looked at me for love. Not my credit rating. I won't mention the race of my new wife (first time married here and I'm so happy!) I can only say, if upwardly mobile bw had my wife's mindset, many would not be single and/or feel the need to broaden their horizons pertaining to dating wm.*
>
> *I was told about this blog from one of my bm single friends. He mentioned it when I asked him why at 39 years old was he still single. He says he isn't even trying to find anyone anymore—the massage parlors in Chinatown are doing him just fine.*
>
> *Sad sad sad.*

☺ Why isn't this *man* off enjoying his new $9.70/hour, '*bad credit* (most likely), *happy*' life with his new wife whose race he won't mention? ☺ Haf mercy! Why is he here seeking attention from bw? And why shouldn't bw broaden their horizons in all respects, whenever they want to or can? Bw have freedom of choice, just like he does.

Actually, I get so many comments like this that I don't post because this is not a comedy blog. The general message from these characters is that since the bw they wanted didn't *'give a brotha a chance,'* they've found a wonderful, beautiful non-bw with a lovely attitude and stacked body, who works everyday, brings home the money to her man, does the housework, does not talk back to him, and performs all kinds of sex at her man's whim, etc.

Mind you, many of these bm don't want *average* looking bw (many of whom would be interested in some of these average and in some cases, way below-average guys). These bm focus mainly on bw who have "the look," which is preferably a bw with the least West African *stereotypical* facial features and hair. Black men of this type tend to complain—and some even become bitter—when the more Euro-looking bw who they prefer, don't want them.

Comments such as this type are therefore masterpieces of trash. However, their comments reveal a lot. These males *crave* attention from bw. Many of them have been telling black women these kinds of fairy tales and the women apparently believed them or allowed themselves to be conned.

My black male cousin (the product of an African father and African-American mom) pointed out that the typical AA man can say the most ridiculous nonsense to other blacks in ordinary conversation (especially to bw), and no one dares to tell him it's rubbish. Since I'm a bw, this is why I'm expected to believe this type of huey. They apparently believe that bw can be categorized as dumb, dumber, and dumbest—since silence is interpreted as agreement.

☺ Methinks they're having massive delusions and are trying to drag me and my bw readership into them. No Thanks!

Okay, here's the *teachable* aspect. Aside from the fact that this relates to a standard plank in the DBR nonsense thought system, we must not overlook that many black girls/women encounter this same type of message in their offline life everyday in one way or the other *if* they mingle much at all with other AAs. This is therefore considered normal thought. They believe these males because they consider this rot they hear to be normal or "the truth."

They, therefore, need to read some of these comments online and have them deconstructed and shredded like the garbage they are. Otherwise, comments such as these raise no alarms and lead many bw to give a non-deserving bm 'a chance' to lead their bw believers over the cliff.

Starting at a very young age, the typical AA female gets tons of *'give a brotha a chance'* messages, and altogether, these and other similar messages ones such as "bw have to work to save our people" *('save alla our people'* in the AA vernacular*)* comprise the biggest part of the anti-bw *indoctrination* program. Once these messages are internalized by the women, they often turn typical American black women into barely-feminine, shrill, loud, aggressive, angry, hardened battleaxes because they, in essence, overburden the women (like mules) with performing the role of the woman *and* the man in the relationship, the family, and in the community.

Many African-American women believe they're saviors or *soldiers* saving people and do not see the need to smile, or learn to flirt, or display typical softer or feminine behavior. They don't even think about it. It's obvious that being a *sista soldier* and simultaneously exhibiting the behavior of a feminine woman is a difficult act to pull off because the behaviors are mutually exclusive. In the dating and mating arena, these aggressive, hardened demeanors do *not* appeal to men of any group. It doesn't surprise me that so many of these women are ultimately left with few viable suitors for marriage or quality fatherhood material for their children.

Not only do numerous bw take on the traditional male role of protector and provider for their children and the community, many think it's their *duty* to provide for, as well as protect and defend black men. They, in effect, become '*shemales.*' Likewise, many of the males display the behavior of self-centered, helpless, dependent children, expecting the women to feed, clothe, and protect them. This is complete role reversal.

Thus, the AA woman *shemale* usually neglects her health, fitness, and often her natural, feminine appearance. Typical males—even the black men they protect and defend—will engage in sex with women of this type and father children by them, but will reject *shemales* as long-term mates because these women don't have the focus or make time to engage in feminine self-care or display typical feminine behavior. In the patriarchal world that we live in, where a woman's value is directly connected to her attractive appearance and feminine behavior, this is why many AA girls and women lose many opportunities to form committed relationships with upwardly mobile men from various groups.

This is how the most damage is done to the psyche and lives of the average AA girl/woman. At the same time that this message is being pounded into her psyche, any positive self esteem she may have is being drained away by various attacks on her appearance, the way she talks, thinks, behaves, dresses, etc.

So she wakes up one morning with her anti-bw indoctrination program embedded in her psyche, and she now considers it to be her identity and the whole truth about her purpose in life as a bw. A major part of this 'truth' is that she must get herself a bm, and practically any bm will do since she has been programmed to *give a (any) brotha a chance.'*

A typical AA woman is unable to figure out which bm is deserving to be given 'a chance' since so many of the males lack the drive to pursue higher education, secure key vocational skills training, won't travel to other places, if necessary, to find employment, or make an attempt to start businesses, etc. Thus, a huge proportion of the males function at a *less-than* level. Also, the woman sees most of the bw in her environment with bm who are not performing their traditional mate or fatherly role or are doing it in a grossly ineffective way.

What seals her fate is that she now *believes* she's worthless, and loveless anyway, and not deserving of much. According to this way of thought, worthless, loveless people don't deserve good people or good things in their lives. So 'da po bm' is just fine for her.

Another part of her new 'truth' is that her identity as a black woman compels her to prop up, lift up, complete, protect, defend, support, and love 'da po bm' *unconditionally.* However, if he becomes totally intolerable, it's okay to replace him, as long as she gets another po' bm. In most AA circles, this is how a card-carrying "black" woman proves that she's 'keepin' it real' and is authentically "black." Many AA women who try to reject this program are quickly labeled as *sellouts, bougie,* or of having *forgotten where they came from,* or not *real* black women.

It's obvious that many AA women do not know how to combat or reject this type of DBR (damaged beyond repair) anti-bw program because she has been programmed from an early age. This is why so many bw continue to make such poor choices in men. These women are under *heavy* pressure to work with the program and never critique it. Dissent is virtually always viewed as 'siding with the enemy' (racist whites) to destroy the black community or helping whites to 'keep a brotha down.'

Remember that when bw know better, most of them *do* better because people do not crash and burn on purpose. When a bw does better, it helps every other black woman. That, in itself, lifts the entire group. I stressed that no black woman should ever be envious/jealous of how well other black women are doing because when any bw is being loved and living well, this is lifting each of us, in the eyes of the world. Just as negativity about black women takes points away from all other bw, positivism about black women *adds* points to all bw too.

Okay, I'll switch gears here to Steven's column (young white male columnist) that will be presented later this week. I know that many of you are eager to get tips on meeting possible dates and mates, but the question you need to ask yourselves is whether you are *prepared* to do what he suggests. Many of his tips will take you out of your comfort zone. Also, do you know how to vet or evaluate men as mate material when you do meet them? This is critical. Click here to read an article from my 'IN OTHER WORDS' blog about how to approach relationships.

Okay, I also want to post a comment below from a 17-year-old young bw. Her sentiments represent tens of thousands (at least) of young bw across this country. You can well see from what she says why my teaching essays and your insightful comments are so vital and can provide at least *some* help. I'm happy that the internet has made it possible for her to connect with us for support and direction.

My name is _____, and I'm a 17-year-old black girl. I don't know if I should be sending this to you at this email address, but this is the only email I could find and I thought that you might be able to help me.

I recently saw a rerun on the Tyra Banks Show talking about race and the mixing of races. On the show was an Asian, white, Mexican, and black female. There were also 2 men that represented each of these races. Tyra then asked the men to pick which female that he found most desirable/ sexy, and none of the men picked the black female. Then Tyra asked them to pick the female they would like most to sleep with. Again, none picked the black girl.

This really makes me want to cry because I am afraid that I won't find some one to love because in honest truth I don't want to marry a black man. And this episode makes me feel that I am really not at all desirable. I haven't had a boyfriend/girlfriend, and this show really makes me insecure. But all I want to know is why black women are so unattractive to society?

This young woman's note made *me* want to cry. This is why the media is so damaging to so many black females. I remember hearing Tyra once say she, too, thought she was too tall, skinny, unattractive, and that she couldn't get a date for her high school prom? Wow! The thing that makes me know that we can combat these spirit-crushing messages successfully is that these messages don't penetrate the psyches of *all* AA women. That's the group that we must study to find out why those same messages didn't get inside them and mess them up. Some of us have been taught or learned a form of immunity to these messages or enough of an immunity to protect us. *All* black females in American society get pretty much the same message—that our beauty and desirability are less-than.

Why is it that those messages don't disable some of us but do so with other black females? Let's all think about this a lot more.

In the meantime, "Live Well!"

Posted by Evia at 8/11/2008 11:00:00 AM

COMMENTS:

Anonymous said...

I know this is unrelated, but Evia, have you thought about putting together an actual Ezine where people can get the blog postings sent to them in an email?

I'm sure that if you looked hard, you would find sponsors. I'm sorry, I just don't have time to come here and read everything, but I know that there is good stuff that I'm missing!

Mon Aug 11, 12:46:00 PM EDT

Miss Pin said...

Your teachable moments from the trolls are truly priceless. ☺ I had my little troll moment this morning when a BM suggested to me that the IR mixers for BW/WM were "not in tune with making a better world or way," and "What about Black men who want to date white, Japanese, Hawaiian or other races?"

Those are the direct quotes, btw. ☺ Uhmm...yea, I can just see this troll showing up to some of the mixers. SMH

There is *no* place BW can get away from these types and as such, we have to be prepared to deal with them.

Sele said...

I'm just gonna zero in on the last email you received, Evia. I know the episode she's talking about because I wrote several letters to the show and expressed how disappointed I was in the topic as well as the guests she picked to represent bw.

I don't care how many awards Tyra receives. She sucks! Her shows are total poison for BW.

Tyra loves to talk about 'good *hair*' and even had Mary J.

Blige on her show expressing how she used to wish she had 'good-hair' when she was a kid. What Tyra needed to do was have a psychiatrist on her show explaining why Mary felt that way while growing up. You'll notice that whenever she has a show about problems in the bc, she always stacks her panel with bw with low self-esteem who end up talking about having problems finding "good" black men or about bw who have problems with bm dating/marrying ww.

Her show is total garbage!

Mon Aug 11, 01:36:00 PM EDT

Glys said...

Nice post, Evia. I understand how the negative images of black women by the media can be damaging to the minds of young black women growing up in American society, but at the same time, these girls need to realize their worth. The statistics which claims 70% of black American women are single, doesn't help either. Sometimes I wish all women thought like me: I absolutely love my looks. Someone making a negative comment about my looks might hurt at first, but I always know that I'm beautiful.

I know that sounds a bit narcissistic, which I am, but look at the positive side: I don't suffer from low self-esteem based on my looks or worse, based on the negative images shown by the media.

The parents of these girls should help them discover their self worth. I grew up in Nigeria, where it isn't too common for parents to tell their kids 'I love you', or 'you are beautiful' like they do in America, but I always knew that they did love me and that I was beautiful to them. As a girl, if you are confident that the people around you (family/friends) love you, that encourages healthier self-esteem. These girls need to learn how to tune out negative images they see, so that it doesn't affect their self-perception

Mon Aug 11, 01:37:00 PM EDT

Glys said...

Oh, and I've had *so many* troll emails. Ha-ha. When you look at my *Myspace* page, it is kind of obvious that I like the vanilla guys. I've got emails from black American men calling me all sorts of names. Apart from names like 'sellout' and 'massa's girl', I find it VERY ANNOYING that I'm considered a 'whore' just because I like white men. If that isn't the definition of a pure ignoramus, then I have no idea what it means. lol.

Mon Aug 11, 01:41:00 PM EDT

Anonymous said...

> I am a bm. Two years ago, I lived in a furnished room. I maked 9.70 an hour and I had (and still own and run) my own repair business on the side. I got married last year to a woman who looked at me for love. Not my credit rating. I won't mention the race of my new wife (first time married here and I'm so happy!) I can only say, if upwardly mobile bw had my wife's mindset, many would not be single and/or feel the need to broaden their horizons pertaining to dating wm.

LOL, what a *"catch"* this loser is. Upwardly mobile BW don't need to *ever* have the mindset of this poor man's wife. Here he is supposedly "happily married" yet he's trolling BW/WM IR blogs. This, in itself, is a sign of an *unhappy* marriage and an unhappy husband. Happy people aren't in others' business.

And for the record, a large percentage of BW who are finally broadening their horizons have *always* preferred white men. It's just been taboo to admit it.

Also, it was a safety issue.

The "bc" is notorious for attempting to silence through ridicule, shunning, even threatening BW with physical violence for publicly expressing interest and preferences for non-BM.

So what we're witnessing today is BW bravely following their hearts—in spite of the possible dangers.

And that's commendable.

> *I was told about this blog from one of my bm single friends. He mentioned it when I asked him why at 39 years old was he still single. He says he isn't even trying to find anyone anymore—the massage parlors in Chinatown are doing him just fine.*
>
> *Sad sad sad.*

Sad indeed. But then again, it's preferable that he sticks to prostitutes (poor dears) than to burden a bw.

Mon Aug 11, 01:44:00 PM EDT

Adelia said...

Thanks again for another great post, Evia! This is the exact reason why I stopped watching Tyra. Yeah, Tyra is doing big things, but when you watch shows like this, it beats down your self-esteem.

I wish Tyra would do a show on bw/wm relationships on how they're thriving. That would be something worth watching.

I remember when I was younger; I had a problem with the way I looked. *I thought* my hair wasn't long enough, I wasn't flirty enough, wasn't light enough, and wasn't showing off my body enough. And one day I said f**k it! I turned off the TV (BET/MTV), turned off the radio, (it's been almost 4 years since I tuned into the radio), stopped buying magazines that said *"do this and that to get the man you want,"* and you know what? I built up my own self-esteem. I did my own thing, wore what I wanted, did my hair the way that suited me, and was careful about what music and magazines I was reading/listening to. And people took notice.

I would suggest the same for this young 17-year-old girl. Click off the TV, and define your own beauty. My cousin right now who is 18 is dating a white guy; black guys were never asking her out, but she was always around white guys.

These trolls are a joke. It must mean we are a force to be reckoned with. For a long time, they believed that bw would wait at home for them. Now they know there's no home for them to go back to. The locks have been changed and there is an alarm system to warn us of dbrbm.

Thank you, Evia, for this blog! And I hope one day when I've met my man, our picture can be put up on this blog.

Mon Aug 11, 01:57:00 PM EDT

Liza said...

> *All black females in American society get pretty much the same message—that our beauty and desirability are less-than.*
> *Why is it that those messages don't disable some of us but do so with other black females? Let's all think about this a lot more.*

Evia, I think one reason why those messages don't disable all of us is because some of us grew up in normal, non-damaged families that served as a "buffer" so to speak. I never had any doubts about my beauty or worth growing up because I had good loving, normal, and affirming men in my immediate family. Father, brother, uncle, Grand fathers, cousins, etc...

Plus, those of us who are lighter-skinned or more "mainstreamed" (less afro-centric) looking had/have our beauty confirmed in the larger society when it comes to the *token black girl.*

This is not fair, but alas, it is still often the case which is unfortunate.

Maybe it's getting a little bit better. I hope so. To be honest, I wouldn't know because I don't watch that much television.

And that's some of the best advice there is. Turn off the TV sometimes and stop supporting those who don't support you back.

Of course, the beauty of black and biracial women of ALL physical types should be recognized and normalized in the American landscape.

This is an obvious 'should.'

But my motto is, if you don't find something in your immediate environment that you find valuable, important, or worthwhile and uplifting to you—for whatever reason, it's your responsibility to *search* for it.

"Seek and you will find." No matter what it is.

Growing up, Donna Summer, Eartha Kitt, Diana Ross, Lena Horne, etc. These black women were my *sheros*. They were (and still are) beautiful, talented, worldly, and all IR-married, at least at some point, and had beautiful families.

I saw the future I could have (happily married, a life filled with travel, successful happy children) in them and researched their backgrounds. I read biographies, because I wanted to see how their minds worked.

Each one of the women I researched had one thing in common: they thought of themselves as *individuals* first.

Human beings, who happened to be women *first* and a color/"race" second, if not last.

I said: *now that's a philosophy I can relate to.*

Those BW who are not a part of these negatives statistics are those who are not afraid to *stand alone* and *apart, if need be,* in order for them to be themselves.

When you really appreciate who you are as an *individual* (and not a part of a *Borg*-like "black community collective"), you can't be any other way. You can stand away and be yourself.

Having friends and associates of a variety of different ethnicities and races helps as well.

Black women simply need to leave the "black" box in their thinking, and in some cases, may need to leave physically if all of the examples of blackness in their immediate environment are damaged.

As for me, I treat all people the same way, according to how they treat me and mine, according to their *behavior.*

And I don't make exceptions for negative/sub standard behavior because someone is labeled "black".

Never have and never will. Because it's nonsensical.

Black women have to stop being so damned afraid of

"ruffling someone's feathers" or "offending" somebody.

They need to ask themselves when was the last time someone walked on eggshells around *them*.

Basically, black women need to start acting in their own best self-interests (and that of their future or present children) and forget anyone who has an issue with that.

Black or otherwise.

Because if someone has an issue with BW doing well, being well, and marrying well, they are an enemy that needs to be defeated.

Mon Aug 11, 02:24:00 PM EDT

Liza said...

So many BW—and black people in general, along with well meaning white liberals—give a "pass" to insane/inappropriate behavior as long as the offender is black (and especially a BM).

Using racism or white supremacy as an excuse.

But IMO, that's a racist response right there. It, in essence, says, "We can't be too hard on them (DBRBM) or expect too much, because they've suffered and therefore we can't expect to them to be up to par and behave civilly/normally."

I say, why not? BM aren't disturbed children in need of coddling/protection. They're grown men who should have to answer for their behavior just like every other man. And they don't hold a monopoly on suffering either.

And BW themselves should be the *first* ones to state that.

The more people make excuses for DBR behavior period, the more it will exist because a problem has to be acknowledged before it can be properly addressed.

Mon Aug 11, 03:21:00 PM EDT

Jewel said...

I can't stand Tyra Banks. She's *no friend to bw*!

And to the young 17-year-old black girl: Hon, don't worry about that silly show. Nine times out of 10, it was set up by Tyra's producers (who were more than likely those who have issues with black women) to make bw feel bad about themselves. Of course Tyra goes along with the okey-dokey cuz she, IMO, is a self-serving mammy in sheep's clothing.

Men are attracted to women. Therefore, a bw who is nice, intelligent and behaves with decorum will have no problem attracting a mate. This happens regardless of her skin shade, hair texture and other trivial criteria that damaged beyond repair black males use to judge bw's beauty by.

Worry not little sister. ☺

Mon Aug 11, 04:03:00 PM EDT

Christine said...

> *I am a bm. Two years ago I lived in a furnished room. I maked 9.70 an hour and I had (and still own and run) my own repair business on the side. I got married last year to a woman who looked at me for love not my credit rating.*

He *"maked"* money. Lord, have mercy. He's a real winner, that one. (rolling eyes)

Mon Aug 11, 05:07:00 PM EDT

Maris said...

Excellent post, Evia, and I know what that 17-year-old is talking about. BW, realize you can't take the media seriously and that's also what needs to be told to our daughters. Tyra Banks *main* audience is WW. This is nothing against WW, but the *last* thing Tyra is gonna do is offend them. That's why she's doing the BW vs BM—knowing good and well we're gonna be dissed, and WW will be put on a pedestal. That's also why, on the episode the 17 year old is talking about, they were not gonna bring beautiful black women like *Sanaa Lathan* or *Gabrielle Union* to the show. I think people were paid for this. Most of these things are staged to appeal to a certain audience.

Didn't that site called *AskMen* vote Beyonce #1 sexiest woman? Didn't all men of all races venerate Lauryn Hill when she was in her prime? Isn't Halle Berry considered perfection? Do we forget Cleopatra and many others? This Tyra Banks episode is a *lie*, ladies. It's a sham! We need to get these girls to realize the media's goal is to program us, shape our perception of reality.

@ Liza

I agree 100% with you! And I can think of Tina Turner too! What a *brave* woman she was!

@ the troll re:

> *I am a bm. Two years ago, I lived in a furnished room. I maked 9.70 an hour and I had (and still own and run) my own repair business on the side. I got married last year to a woman who looked at me for love. Not my credit rating. I won't mention the race of my new wife (first time married here and I'm so happy!)*

You've been married for the first time, huh? Yet she's your "new" wife? Don't people say "new" when they had an "ex"? Guess your story is BS. You ain't gotta lie, Craig.

Mon Aug 11, 05:39:00 PM EDT

Deidre said...

I've heard of this book, but haven't read it yet, but I like what Spangler stated on her 'About Page.'

http://www.theprincessformula.com/about.htm

"Although women like independence, they also want to be taken care of by their mate ...they want someone who is stronger than themselves ... Independent women don't want to take care of their men, they don't want to split expenses. They can have a roommate for that."

I also read a part in Ginie Sayles book about a woman who was dating a guy and they only ever went out to lunch. Well anyway, he would have her pay for lunch, saying he left his wallet at home. He even had the gall to pull out empty pockets. She found out unbeknownst to him that he was dating another women and he was paying for the dinner dates, but yet not hers. He was basically saving money with this chick so he could spend it on the other one on dinner dates. Anyway, during a lunch date, she ordered a big meal and so did he and then told him she need to leave to make a phone call and left his ass with the tab.lol

And to the dbr men all around the world: take heed.

http://www.nriworld.in/news/689-Bride-beats-groom-badly-after-he-refuses-to-marry-her-with-strange-reason

Kudos to that girl for having the guts to stand up for herself and for her family doing the same.

Mon Aug 11, 06:48:00 PM EDT

Lynda said...

My husband coaches at a swim club in the suburbs of a major east coast city. Because of his position, we are given membership status. What this means is that my daughter is usually the only AA among many swimmers.

Every summer, the club sponsors a teen party. Although she is not yet a teen, the teen party is open to anyone entering middle school.

So, one Sunday night, she goes to the teen party with such great anticipation. When my husband picked her up after the party ended, she was in tears. Her remark: "Who wants to dance with the ugly, fat, Black girl." She is not fat; however, she is very developed for a 12-year-old. And, she is considered beautiful by many strangers who have approached me, however, her peers give her no attention.

As a mom, I find that I have to do a lot of damage control. Your web site has been extremely helpful in that matter. I am teaching her to value herself and accept only someone who values her. That is my mantra.

Mon Aug 11, 07:37:00 PM EDT

Sherry said...

> I don't care how many awards Tyra receives. She sucks majorly. Her shows are total poison for BW.

Sele, yes! Critical thinking most definitely involves *not* watching her show. She is like the BF Jerry Springer, except unwatchable, and I was so annoyed to see her "dressed up" as Michelle Obama.

I truly don't think she realizes how far reaching she is, including into the very *minds* of black women, and herein lies the true destruction.

Mon Aug 11, 07:57:00 PM EDT

Anonymous said...

> The "bc" is notorious for attempting to silence through ridicule, shunning, even threatening BW with physical violence for publicly expressing interests and preferences for non-BM.

Like that poor girl whose bm friends beat her up for saying she thought a white athlete was cute.

> I haven't had a boyfriend/girlfriend, and this show really makes me insecure. But all i want to know is why are black women so unattractive to society?

> I don't care how many awards Tyra receives. She sucks! Her shows are total poison for BW.

Big reason I don't watch her show. If I want black empowerment from a black woman, I watch Oprah. I might not agree with everything she says, but at least I don't feel like shit when it's over. Her shows make me wanna do something, whereas Tyra's just make me feel depressed. At least Oprah gets someone on there to talk about why people feel certain ways about themselves, or do things to themselves or others.

I watched Tyra's show once/maybe twice and that was it. I know bw/am couples she pissed off with the episode of the bw who only married her Asian husband so her kids would be light with so called *good hair*. The woman didn't realize this at the time, but she shows a black man with an Indian women and that story is told as an endearment of how love conquers all, racism, etc. See the positive spin. But the bw married to the Asian man married him supposedly because of low self-esteem issues. Stop!

Way to go Tyra. You date out while you tell/make other bg/bw feel unloved and unwanted. At least Ananda tried to be more balanced, but that's probably why her show was cancelled.

> . . . but at the same time, these girls need to realize their worth. The statistics which claims 70% of black American women are single, doesn't help either.

You know I listened to *Antonio Thornton* at work one day. This guy is great. Anyway, he said something that I know I should have known, but didn't think of it. I have been studying the law of attraction, and one thing he noted was when he thought no one would want to talk to him at a convention he was attending, no one talked or ate with him etc. until he got his mind right. His friend gave him some advice about that, a little tough love. He changed his thinking and ended up sitting with the big whigs at the convention.

And then I thought about it. If I say that men don't find me attractive, then they won't, because I don't believe that men find me attractive. In other words, I don't feel I have worth and people sense that like the plague. So, it's also how you think of yourself and what you put out there. I'm still learning to change my thinking, especially when images or something someone says might linger in my psyche a little too long.

> Oh and I've had so many troll emails. ha-ha. When you look at my Myspace page, it is kind of obvious that I like the vanilla guys. I've got emails from black American men calling me all sorts of names. Apart from names like 'sellout' and 'massa's girl', I find it VERY ANNOYING that I'm considered a 'whore' just because I like white men. If that isn't the definition of a pure

ignoramus, then I have no idea what it means.
lol.

Funny how you can go to these same black men's/boys' *Myspace/Facebook* pages etc., and see nothing, but Asian, White, nonblack women, but no bw, or if they're there, they look like hoochies. And that's another thing I want to tell these girls. Stop that mess. Stop putting *hoochiefied* pictures on their profile! lol It is *so* self-sabotaging.

Turn the TV off, and yes, the internet too. But also know that you have more and different media at your disposal. Seek out alternatives.

Because of the internet, you can now watch shows that you choose. I watch shows online like *Doctor Who* or Indie shows like *Sanctuary* (Scifi channel picked it up). I also read at *Monster Zero Productions*. The point is that sometimes you have to change your media outlet as well. Plus, it's inspiring how you have internet shows like *Prom Queen, After World,* etc. because it means that the sky's not the limit.

I know some blacks who think I'm weird, but I get IR books of bw in relationships with other race men. I watch movies like *Unbowed*. Whew! Girls, you gotta check out that movie just for the black woman-interracial pairing 'cause that dude is hot! Also, watch *The Missing* (not IR, but he's in it and hot), *Strange Days, Catfish in Black Bean Sauce,* etc. Sometimes you have to do this to keep up the positive thinking when others would put you down.

> *I did my own thing, wore what I wanted,*
> *did my hair the way that suited me, and was*
> *careful about what music and magazines I was*

reading/listening to. And people took notice.

I know what you mean because I'm learning that just because it's *soul* doesn't mean it's any better than R&B and Hip Hop. A lot of the *Neo Soul* music was some of the most damaging, jacked-up songs I have heard—like a song telling women to rescue a man. I was thinking why don't you go and rescue *her*--you loser? That song is just as bad as the song that says, *"She got her own house, she got her own car, she working two jobs,"* etc. Sorry for the rant.

Mon Aug 11, 09:09:00 PM EDT

Wanda said...

> *Because if someone has an issue with BW doing well, being well, and marrying well, they are an enemy that needs to be defeated.*

Now you said that! That is the quote of the century! I am putting that on a t-shirt!

Mon Aug 11, 09:24:00 PM EDT

Glys said...

> *So many BW—and black people in general, along with well meaning white liberals—give a "pass" to insane/inappropriate behavior as long as the offender is black (and especially a BM).*
> *Using racism or white supremacy as an excuse.*

I agree *somewhat* with this comment by Liza. I notice a lot of blacks in the USA blame whites for everything and tend to use slavery as an excuse for everything.

As an example, I made a response to a video on *YouTube* titled: "White Men Hate Black Women." This user had posted a video of a racist white man who appeared on the *Tyra* show and used that as an example of how *all* white men feel about black women. ☺ I tried to reason with this person that there are close-minded, ignorant people in every group and that they can't use examples of crimes committed centuries ago during slavery (by white men against black women) to prove that *all* or even typical white men in this generation would hate black women. Since I date white men and defended the men I've dated, he accused me of *'hating my own race'* and of being a *'mammy.'* LOL

If you go to *YouTube*, there are countless videos (and comments on these videos) that are made to put down the beauty of black women. I notice *a lot* of these videos are made by black American men, which is extremely disturbing, in my opinion. I can only hope that those young black girls who watch such videos know how to tune out such negativity. I've never seen or heard an African man do this. African men will praise the beauty of their women *first.* lol. It really is sad. SMH

Mon Aug 11, 10:14:00 PM EDT

Sele said...

> *At least Ananda tried to be more balanced, but that's probably why her show was cancelled.*

OMG! I remember that show. I guess it went the same way *Mother Love*'s show did.

Mon Aug 11, 11:18:00 PM EDT

Sele said...

> *Tyra is like the BF Jerry Springer, except unwatchable, and I was so annoyed to see her "dressed up" as Michelle Obama.*

Sherry, I thought I was the only one that thought she looked plain, damn ridiculous.

Mon Aug 11, 11:20:00 PM EDT

Ephy said...

I just want to take this opportunity to mention how I can't stand Tyra. I know she is a fellow bw, but she is doing more harm than good to all of us. Why is she going out of her way to prove what other people already think? She, herself, is downgrading us with her million and one issues. Believe it or not, not all bw have issues with their hair; however, from her show, you would think bw are crying themselves to sleep every night just thinking about their hair.

Also, I'm sure her guests are not picked off the street; she interviews them and picks who is going to be more controversial. If she's not the one choosing her guest, then WTH! What's the point of the *Tyra Banks Show*? Why is she doing this to us? Moreover, do y'all know young white women *love* her show and can y'all really blame them? I would also love a show, as a ww, where there's a bw with her long flowing fake "hair" constantly talking about her hair issues and proving to me that I'm more desirable than her. Tyra simply sucks.

Tue Aug 12, 02:28:00 AM EDT

Hsa said...

Re the 17-year-old, I think we are looking at it with mature eyes and with hindsight. Many of us grew up before this wholesale attempt to make bw an 'unloved class'. I remember when *Ricky Lake* started up her mess, how angry and humiliated as a bw I felt with the continuous parading of bw disgracing themselves over bm/ww (so much so that now the definition of 'opposers to IR' is bw, in the popular view). I was hardly a teenager and had had years of reinforced self-esteem to be able to eventually put this trash where it really belonged—in the garbage.

It's all good and well to say *turn it off*, but what about girls who haven't got to the point of understanding media but think because it is said on TV, it is true? Let's face it—we were all there at one point.

This shows me how much of a life and death situation this is now. There is a battle for the souls of black girls. On one side, there are those who want to destroy them or keep them in a class where they can be easily used, aka a slave class (America has always had a need for a slave class), and on the other, those who are trying to fight back. I know where I stand!

Supposing I wanted to Date a White Guy...? [website]

Tue Aug 12, 02:33:00 AM EDT

Ephy said..

> *And, she is considered beautiful by many strangers who have approached me, however, her peers give her no attention.*
> *As a mom, I find that I have to do a lot of damage control. Your web site has been extremely helpful in that matter. I am teaching her to value herself and accept only someone who values her. That is my mantra.*

Her peers are not giving her any attention because at that age, they're even more receptive to societal cues about desirability. Like I've said before, watch Disney channel for a day and you'll see the message loud and clear about whose hot and who's not. Why should black girls be the '*not*'?

I know the episode she's talking about because I wrote several letters to the show and expressed how disappointed I was in the topic as well as the guests she picked to represent bw.

Like my mother always says, "Tyra's an idiot." Hate to be so harsh, but y'all, she deserves it. No matter how good we feel about ourselves, because we're human, we're always going to care about what other human beings think about us. She is lowering and degrading us. I'm definitely going to copy Sele and write this annoying woman a piece of my mind. I think we all should. The thing that actually irritates me the most about her is that she does this under the guise that she cares about black girls' self-esteem. Did she lose her mind? When did providing "proof" that black females are undesirable become an uplifting gesture?

Tue Aug 12, 02:59:00 AM EDT

Tanya said...

Didn't that site called AskMen vote Beyonce #1 sexiest woman? Didn't all men of all races venerate Lauryn Hill when she was in her prime? Isn't Halle Berry considered perfection? Do we forget Cleopatra and many others? This Tyra Banks episode is a lie, ladies. It's a sham! We need to get these girls to realize the media's goal is to program us, shape our perception of reality.

Holding up Beyonce and Halle as examples of black beauty is insulting, don't ya think? How can you tell a black girl that she is beautiful and desirable by pointing to women who look nothing like her? Halle may not be so bad, but Beyonce?

I agree about Lauryn though; she has a gorgeous face.

Tue Aug 12, 03:48:00 AM EDT

Maris said...

> *Holding up Beyonce and Halle as examples*
> *of black beauty is insulting, don't ya think? . . . .*

How is that insulting? Because they're not dark-skinned? What is so wrong about celebrating our diversity as bw? Is it insulting to call Alicia Keys a beautiful sister just like we call Iman a beautiful sister? I don't know the complexion of our 17-year-old little sister, that's the reason why I have listed women with different skin shades. I will not play the *divide game* when it comes to sisterhood. I am aware of the colorism issue in the black community, but our lighter sisters have their own problems too.

I have young girls in my family—teens like this 17 year old—who have Beyonce's complexion and have self-esteem issues because of this society. Their hair is considered too nappy, or because they're not black enough to some, or because they're "black, *unfortunately*" to other people, or their skin is being fetishized by some DBRbm (like Yung Berg) and they suffer from this. Heck, Beyonce, herself, has self-esteem issues.

Tyra Banks, who is nowhere near Lauryn's complexion, is the *epitome* of self-esteem issues! Halle is known for tanning because she doesn't feel black enough!

That's why, no matter how divisive people try to be with the skin shade thing, I am behind *all* my sisters!

Yes we have beautiful dark-skinned sisters like Liyah Kebede, Tomiko Frasier, Kelly Rowland, Alek Wek, Iman, Naomi and I could go on and on, but what I wanted to do was to purposely choose dark (Lauryn), brown (Halle), light (Beyonce) to represent all shades. I instantly thought of Lauryn for dark-skinned sisters because she had the world at her feet.

Also, my point with Beyonce was that she was listed above *all* the WW who are said to be the sexiest women on the planet. Regardless of her skin shade, it's not Paris Hilton who got the #1 spot. And my point with Halle is that she's considered perfection when the world is saying blond-haired, blue-eyed women are supposedly perfect, and she looks *nothing* like a blond-haired, blue-eyed girl.

I don't see anything insulting about my comment!

Tue Aug 12, 08:40:00 AM EDT

Berona said...

Since the discussion on talk shows is moving along, has anyone thought of starting a mailing campaign to these networks? For example, we collect their mailing addresses or email addresses, and those with blogs can leave them on the sidebar for readers to write to them. If there is a problem where BW are denigrated, we can all be alerted and we begin to write and email in—several times.

So say there is a problem with the Tyra show, we all do a mass mail-in right after the aired episode and do this each time on whichever show or movie that we believe is denigrating to bw. Of course, we'd provide as many details as necessary to make the point.

Tue Aug 12, 09:20:00 AM EDT

Art said...

The period we're in now is a period in which many AA women are trying to learn the steps

> *they need to use to both access and take advantage of all their options. This period will henceforth be known as 'the quiet before the stampede.'*

I'm beginning to think the growth in bw/wm IRs is more than a straight-line increase. It well could be a kind of exponential gain that feeds off its own increase; where the increase line is always curving upward. It might be interesting to see what the numbers say ... hmm ...

Tue Aug 12, 11:08:00 AM EDT

Spring said...

> *So say there is a problem with the Tyra show, we all do a mass mail-in right after the aired episode . . . .*

We should start doing this whenever we have issues with the media and their handling of our image.

Tue Aug 12, 11:09:00 AM EDT

Evia said...

> *Holding up Beyonce and Halle as examples of black beauty is insulting, don't ya think? How can you tell a black girl that she is beautiful and desirable by pointing to women who look nothing like her? Halle may not be so bad, but Beyonce? . . . .*

I think you need to elaborate on this issue because some of us may be misinterpreting you. That's easy to do on these boards.

Many black women look at these women through the color-struck eyes of many others in the bc or *the average bm*. In a sexist, patriarchal world, it is largely men who determine the value of women and men largely based this on a woman's attractiveness or lack of it. Attractiveness, in the eyes of *most* black men, is inextricably linked to a woman's complexion, the overwhelming most of the time. Women tend to view themselves, their value, and that of other women through the eyes of men. This is *internalized sexism.* This is the same as many non-white people who view themselves, their value, and that of other nonwhite people through the eyes of racist whites. That is called *internalized racism.* So, the average bw is hit with racism and sexism from outside herself *plus* her own internalized racism and internalized sexism.

To a typical wm who appreciates the beauty of bw, the difference between the complexions of these bw mentioned is not an issue because they are *all* "black" women to the *average* white guy—if you're simply talking about their complexions, which it seems that you are. Yes, there are preferences in some cases among wm for chocolate, butterscotch, or *cafe au lait* complexions, but I would bet that the preferences pretty much average out and all skin shades of bw would be just fine—among wm who like bw's beauty. There is much evidence to show that if there actually is a preference, the average wm who is attracted to bw would prefer the darker bw. However, this is in stark contrast to typical AA men whose preference would be skewed *heavily* towards lighter bw.

As I'd pointed out, I noticed years ago how more AA men would express interest in me in the wintertime but not nearly as many would show any interest in me in the summertime. ☺ My skin is several shades lighter in the wintertime, of course. That's the *only* difference. I don't believe I would've experienced this with many, if any, wm at all.

Only black—or in my experience, it's overwhelmingly mostly *AA folks*—who split hairs about how much lighter or darker this black person is than that one and how this bw has "*good*" hair or a "*better* grade" of hair. I've heard AAs get into detailed discussions about a bw's long hair, or about which bw is wearing a weave vs her natural hair or whether she has a *bone-straight* relaxer in her hair, and yadda, yadda.

Oprah actually devoted a portion of one of her shows to *prove* that most of her hairstyles consist of her own hair. She yanked on her naturally longer hair on her show to prove it was hers! Still, I heard some bw saying that Oprah was lying. So much ado about hair! SMH

That's proof positive of the damage done by internalized sexism and racism. It's apparent that most women in the world believe now that more hair of a certain more Euro-looking type gives women an advantage in competing for men. Culturally speaking, hair plays multiple roles. In comparing what is considered sexually alluring in some cultures versus others, having *more* hair is considered alluring to the opposite sex in *some* cultures much more than in others. Even men wear toupees or get hair implants to get more hair in order to compete for women in some parts of the world. ☺

But none of this started with bw. Wigs, weaves, hairpieces, etc. were not invented or mass-produced for bw. Bw in the West are only a chunk of the worldwide purchasers of mass-produced hair or hair enhancements. Yet *only* bw (or I should say, AA women and similar bw) seem to receive the most criticism for wearing fake hair. This criticism is mainly from other blacks. I'd say it's because AA women have high visibility on the world stage. They also are the main or largest group of bw who are at the intersection of racism and sexism.

This hair and complexion obsession has become a virtual science among some AAs. It *traumatizes* certain black girls and bw, but not *all* of us. It's critical to point out that *some* of us bw do not cooperate with this spirit-crushing program. We are aware and have sufficient self-esteem to not be victims of the traps of external or internalized sexism or racism, and thus, do not obsess or feel trauma regarding our complexion or hair. We know our beauty and worth. We may be the *fortunate few*, but we exist.

The vast majority of wm who like bw don't care about our *grade* of hair at all. I don't know exactly how to get this across to bw, but a relative few white people are even aware of these *grades* of black hair. The average wm only cares about whether the hairstyle looks good on us—long or short, natural or straight. And believe it or not, many wm who like bw don't care whether our hair came out of our scalps or whether it came from the salon or store. It's only a hair "style" to them, which can be changed. Our "worth" is not connected with our hair to the average one of them—the way it is with many bm.

I have never experienced hair or complexion *trauma*. As a black girl and woman, my complexion was considered light *enough*. Ever since my young adult years, I've worn my hair in mostly natural hairstyles: braids, twists, and for a brief time in an "afro." I escaped the jeers from other AAs because I barely mingled with the types of AAs who consider my naturally-coiled hair to be offensive. Not saying that most blacks don't think about it sometimes, but there are segments of AAs (and similar blacks) who have made hair and skin shade into a pseudo religion. They are hair and skin shade *maniacs*. It's an illness of a sort. They make critical life decisions about other black people based mostly on the hair and skin shade of those other blacks. They don't see anything wrong with that and will instead rationalize it by saying they were taught by the white media to think that way, and so be it. They brush off the damage it does to themselves and other blacks, and many of this group talk constantly about how "black" they are. SMH

In the U.S., this type of fixation on hair and complexion comes mainly from certain elements of AAs. If you're not around them much, you don't experience it. My natural hair has been accepted (or never mentioned) and even complimented quite often by the whites and others I've mingled with. I do realize hair and complexion issues cause *pain* for many bw and this is why I talk about both of those. However, to me, complexion discrimination among blacks is a much bigger issue because a person can change/hide their hair but not their complexion.

Complexion discrimination among some segments of blacks is about as foul as things can get because if another black person devalues a darker person due to their dark skin shade, this interferes with those two black people moving along together in a positive way. It causes friction and divisiveness. How well can you work together with another person if you can't stand the way they look or devalue the skin they're in?

But to many other AAs, this is just business as usual. ☹

They never consider how this issue eats away at black cohesiveness and development. It's never an agenda item on the list at those "*Black State of the Union*" fanfares.

However, on the IR dating and mating front, a black woman's skin shade is largely insignificant to the average white guy who likes black women. Many wm even *prefer* darker bw. Outside of Hollywood casting, wm don't hunt and peck among bw to find a light-skinned, Euro looking bw with Euro features because if that were important to them romantically, they'd just find a ww. We are *all* much darker to them. We are often considered "exotic" in a positive way to some of these guys.

Differences in skin shades, facial features, accents, customs, etc. are often viewed as exotic in a positive way to others. When I lived in Nigeria, some people viewed me as exotic. They liked to hear me talk. ☺

@ Berona

> *Since the discussion on talk shows is moving along, has anyone thought of starting a mailing campaign to these networks? . . . .*

Great idea! Why don't you set this up and tell us how it works.

Tue Aug 12, 11:22:00 AM EDT

Jewel said...

I agree with Maris. Light-skinned bw are still *black*. Trying to split hairs and argue otherwise is divisive and keeps bw in a marginalized position. We have to stick together.

Besides, it's not light-skinned bw's fault that dbr-black males continue to act like caged monkeys over them.

Tue Aug 12, 11:47:00 AM EDT

Evia said...

> *I'm beginning to think the growth in bw/wm IRs is more than a straight-line increase. It well could be a kind of exponential gain that feeds off its own increase; where the increase line is always curving upward. It might be interesting to see what the numbers say ... hmm ...*

For real! Art, we are on the brink of a mass exodus of bw to *quality* non-bm due to sheer numbers. This is why many bw come to my blog and similar ones. They're trying to get tips on how exactly to do the "mating dance" with QLL wm and other non-bm. LOL! The mating dance is quite different with a wm than with a bm. And some wm have told me that the mating dance with bw is quite different than with ww and Asian women.

At any rate, at one point soon, wm and bw will both learn the necessary steps and there will be an explosion of bw-wm/bw-nonbm relationships and marriages. Bw are very resourceful. Throughout history, bw have always found a way. They will find a way in this case too because many wm, like yourself, are also ready and eager to do their part. So, it's only a matter of time before the dam breaks.

Tue Aug 12, 11:47:00 AM EDT

Miss Pin said...

> *The mating dance is quite different with a wm than with a bm.*

I think this is the biggest hurdle a lot of BW have. I think we have to let go of our *tradition* of being approached. We are going to have to step out of our comfort zone and let other men know we find them attractive and we are open/available to them.

For a lot of us, this is new and in some instances, scary; we are afraid of rejection, being taken as "loose," etc. But, I think it is going to come down to: do it or just exist *as is*. Some will say it's not *fair* that we have to do so much of the work, but life isn't fair and we can stay stuck on that, or do what has to be done to move forward.

Tue Aug 12, 11:57:00 AM EDT

Berona said...

Hey Evia, I will do so. ☺ Just wanted to see where everyone was with it. I will set it on the side bar of my blog. If anyone knows of any snail mail addresses to NBC, ABC, CBS, MTV, BET or magazines, and so on, *pleeease* let me know and let all of us know who have blogs.

Basically, this mass mail campaign is alert-based. When something is "spotted," it should be reported.

I would call it a kind of "Watchwoman" job.

If a Tyra show or some other show airs an unsatisfactory episode about bw, it should be reported on all blogs and readers should be asked to mail/email the show. If the same show re-airs, then write them again until they get message.

A kind of *Watchwoman Alert*.

Those who may be members of *Blogger* or another blogging system but who may not blog can participate by simply posting up the concern to date and the emails and addresses to which one may write.

Think of *Lord of the Rings* (*Return of the King*?) when they were lighting the fires to alert everyone of the approaching enemy.

Tue Aug 12, 01:19:00 PM EDT

Berona said...

I forgot to mention that the WM can participate in this action too, especially when it comes to disrespect of BW/WM unions.

Tue Aug 12, 01:21:00 PM EDT

Maggie said...

> *I think this is the biggest hurdle a lot of BW have. I think we have to let go of our tradition of being approached. We are going to have to step out of our comfort zone and let other men know we find them attractive and we are open/available to them.*

I agree and I think this is *key*. I think what BW must learn is how to approach men without actually approaching them.

I guess I'm old fashioned and I don't think that women should approach men directly. From my own experiences, that's never worked well. From what I've observed through other women, it doesn't work as well either. There are ways of letting a man know that you are interested in him and that you want him to approach you without actually "approaching" him. Men may say something different in regard to this matter, but I've learned from watching *them* that what they say and what they actually do are sometimes two very different things. lol

Tue Aug 12, 01:26:00 PM EDT

Evia said...

> *I think this is the biggest hurdle a lot of BW have. I think we have to let go of our tradition of being approached. . . . .*

On point! Miss Pin, this is exactly what's got to happen until the "new" word gets out there that bw are really and truly interested in wm and other non-bm. Many wm cannot believe that lots of bw are interested in them because they've heard so much that bw are diehards for bm. And let's face it, from what I observe, many bw don't act exactly friendly towards wm.

Unfortunately, there aren't the usual avenues for bw to get the "new" word out there. *ESSENCE* isn't saying it at this point; *Ebony Magazine* isn't either, and *Oprah* only did a show or two about bw-wm dating and marriage. I think they fear that black community would devour them if they did. We know that many in the bc would rather for bw to be unloved and unmarried than to be with wm. Many don't say that, but watch their *actions*.

The white magazines and media won't do it because the backlash would be ferocious from the white and black communities. Advertising revenues would take a hit.

This is why our blogs are popular and necessary. When you really think about it, our blogs aren't really saying much of anything, except that we talk about what lots of bw really feel— not what they claim to feel. I would say that most bw *claim* to other blacks that they're not interested in wm because they don't want to be accused of *betraying* bm or they want to avoid the label of 'sellout.' (Isn't it interesting how most bm don't care about that when they date and marry non-bw?)

However, the *real* deal is that the overwhelming portion of sensible bw are very definitely interested in a quality, lovable and loving mate, irrespective of his complexion, race, ethnicity, etc.

The media is not talking about this scorching hot topic but

there's a *lot* of interest in it. The intersection of race and sex is about the hottest place in town, yet neither the mainstream media nor any of the top magazines or newspapers will touch it—even though their ratings would shoot through the roof. Some people are confused about why the media barely talks about bw-wm relationships. I know that it's mostly due to the "money trail." Money is usually behind any social situation that seems unfathomable.

What I'm saying is that bw should welcome it but cannot *depend* on any publicity about this issue from the black or white media. *We* have to become the media concerning *us*, and we must vocally *and* otherwise support other bw regarding broadening their dating and marriage pool. We also should support any media or advertising that highlights quality bw-non-bm interactions. Let them know we appreciate them.

On another note, one of the things that we need to address is some of the attitudes and behaviors that *some* black women display: they blab unsavory things about themselves and "act out" in many public scenarios. *All* bw pay a price for these "acting out" bw because the perception is that it's the way bw (as a group) think, act, and *are*. Unfortunately, so many AA women of certain demographics believe that "acting out" (loudness, coarseness, clowning, aggressiveness, rudeness, roughness, sour attitudes, extreme hairstyles and attire, general uncouthness, etc.) is *acting black*.

This is why some of us are now advocating that bw who plan to have normal lives and those who want to 'Live Well' are going to have to set themselves apart from the *acting black crew* (ABCs) of bw and bm. Get away from them. This is really critical. It is the only chance that many bw have because the acting black crew is an ugly segment of AAs that no one wants around them. Many of them don't even want to be around each other, but have no choice. Some of them believe that *acting black gives them a separate identity from whites,* and they take pride in that. Others copy the behavior to feel accepted or simply don't know any better. Either way, it has become a type of security blanket for a lot of insecure AAs who are unaware of their actual *identity*. It's a form of amnesia. It's only other AAs who know that many of these folks are "acting." ☺

Bw cannot prevent other bw from "acting black," but each bw can separate or distance herself from the "acting black" crew in practically any situation, or she can do it as much as possible.

For ex., Darren and I were at a *McDonald's* restaurant a couple of weeks ago in a major city and a bw near us was talking loudly to her girlfriend who sat at another table. It was the lunch hour, and the place was crowded. People were looking for seats, yet these women sat at separate tables talking in blaring voices to each other. No one wanted to get near them. And what they were saying was not exactly lunchtime conversation either. They took the time to eye me and Darren though—watched every move we made! ☺

Uncouth behavior by women in any culture or society is a turnoff to men. Even many men of that same type don't want uncouth women, if they have a choice. And likewise, no sensible woman wants an uncouth man.

If there were quality men there who might have been interested in them, they would have lost interest and *fast*!

Bw *must* behave with decorum! Even if they were never taught to do it, they can learn. The reward is well worth it!

Anyway, when we saw a couple of empty seats away from where they were sitting, we got up and moved away. These bw were dressed nicely, had cute hairdos, and some men would have considered them attractive.

This is something I never thought about—up until three years ago because I didn't know many of the things I know now about the social scene for many AAs. I never thought much about the issues that I write about these days. Of course, I knew there were certain issues between AA men and women, but I figured at that point that most bw had the man she wanted or was at least okay with him, or with being alone. Whew! So much has changed. At a time when I'd bet that at least 50% of the 70% of un-partnered bw are praying to meet a compatible man of quality, it's very bad for business when bw *perform* in a public arena like that.

The good news is that the bulk of AA women are not like that. The bad news is that the minority of bw of that type have such distasteful behavior until they overshadow the rest of us.

This is a hot issue because bw don't like to hear that they need to do any more changing. The fact is that some bw have attitudes and behaviors that would turn off virtually any quality man. Many of these attitudes and behavior fall into the *acting black* category.

Those of us without amnesia must make the effort to distinguish ourselves from the ABCs in every facet of life that we can manage—the way we talk, walk, how we dress, where we go, live, shop, etc. I always behave with decorum, in public. Aside from that being my natural behavior, I certainly don't want to ever be mistaken for an uncouth woman. Prejudiced strangers might think I'm uncouth when they first see/meet me, but I'm not going to prove it to them.

When it comes to meeting quality men, those *acting black* women don't normally go to places where there are lots of non-bm or pursue hobbies and activities that those men take part in. If you want to meet men of that type, you've got to go to those places. You're going to have to make it a habit of getting within a few feet of men of that sort from whichever background and be friendly, lighthearted, and receptive, possibly ask for help with something or ask for information as a conversation starter or make a comment.

If one of these guys shows no interest or rejects you, he doesn't know you; so don't take it personally. You don't know what's going on his life; stop thinking that it's always about *you*. Flutter your wings and continue to mingle.

I'll put on my *comparative cultures* hat here. Those of us black women who make it a point to behave *normally*—which means behaving within the established, worldwide, standard norms—cannot stop those ABCs and assorted other blacks from acting like black caricatures. Normal behavior has nothing to do with *acting white*. Behaving with decorum is the norm *everywhere,* in societies throughout the world.

It is segments of AAs who attribute the "moderate" style of behavior that many mainstream whites display as "acting white," but this is *not* a white thing. Moderate behavior is a spectrum of normal, customary behavior that the vast majority of people display—from Sub-Saharan Africa to the North Pole. It is the predominant behavior displayed by people of *all* ethnicities and races, and since the time of recorded history. Ill-mannered, disruptive, clowning behavior is anti-social behavior. It is abnormal. It is *not* authentic AA or African cultural behavior. If you spend time around born and bred Africans or in an African cultural milieu or even *old school* AAs (like me) for more than a minute, you will quickly see that we all "act white" (according to the ABCs) because our behavior is *normal* behavior. Period.

Tue Aug 12, 02:37:00 PM EDT

Liza said...

> *This is why some of us are now advocating that bw who plan to have normal lives and those who want to 'Live Well' are going to have to set themselves apart from the "acting black" type of bw and bm. Get away from them. This is really critical. It is the only chance that many bw have because the acting black crew is an ugly segment of AAs. . . .*

Right! That's what I've been saying all along. It's wonderful how we're all observing the same thing. It is *vital* to remove yourself from their presence. Because fair or not, they reflect badly on us *all*.

It's best to disassociate ASAP and this can be done in nearly every situation. Calmly and coolly.

> *Bw cannot prevent other bw from "acting black," but each bw can separate or distance herself from the "acting black" crew in practically any situation, or she can do it as much as possible.*

BW who wish to present themselves in the best, most intelligent, and attractive light, need to do it *every* time. And keep their children away from their negative influence too.

Tue Aug 12, 03:07:00 PM EDT

Anonymous said...

> *If you go to YouTube, there are countless videos (and comments on these videos) that are made to put down the beauty of black women. I notice a lot of these videos are made by black American men, which is extremely disturbing in my opinion. I can only hope that those young black girls who watch such videos know how to tune out such negativity. I've never seen or heard an African do this. African men will praise the beauty of their women first. lol. It really is sad. SMH*

Big reason I go to *Slowalker700 Love,* the *Black Faces* series. He has videos showing African/black women. I look these types of videos up and post them in my 'black people around the world' folder. And when I find black men who praise bw, I bookmark that there as well. I try to avoid the ignorant videos, but sometimes you need to know who the fools are out there. Other than that, I don't watch too many of them. Way too damaging. I also try not to check out the posts unless they are positive. If they're negative, I just watch the videos because there is no use talking to a fool.

> *My natural hair has been accepted (or never mentioned) and even complimented quite often by the whites and others I've mingled with.*

You know, I have had Ethiopian, Eritrean, and Somali men and women speak to me in their language and then I have to tell them that I don't speak the language. I want to learn the languages though. This one ww on the bus asked me if I was Eritrean. She said that I resembled the many men and women there (she lived there with her family for years. I think her dad was an Anthropologist or something like that). She most def found America to be weird in its beauty standards even though she herself is American.

I'm not what others consider *light*-skinned, but more caramel. When I was younger, and even still a little today, I wanted to have my mother's skin tone that is darker than mine. My mother always taught me that I had my own beauty and not to feel like I was *less than* because I didn't look like someone else. She said that she had to work on her esteem issues about being a dark-skinned woman in an all-black environment. She even had family calling and asking for the darkest one and guys telling her she's beautiful, but they don't do *darkies,* and etc.

I never knew this because she always held herself in high regard. Basically, she said it hurt a few times, but then she'd ask them, '*Why the hell did you come to dance with me or talk to me if you don't do darkies as you say?*' Had them speechless. She doesn't put up with that foolishness.

Oh, and on the hair thing—do what you want. I have been learning to debunk black hair care myths. Half the mess about black peoples' hair is false. The thing is: experiment. Do what works for you. I've learned I can actually—*gasp!*—wash my hair everyday without losing so-called *natural oils*. (My aunt told me we don't have natural oils. I was like, "Well then, we wouldn't have hair.") When my aunt told me that black hair can't be washed as often and dirt and oil make the hair grow, and that's why bw should only wash our hair once or twice a month. I knew better. I had done my own research. I had experimented with different things for myself, read other peoples' experiences. And yes, some things don't work for some people.

Tue Aug 12, 03:45:00 PM EDT

Evia said...

> *I know this is unrelated, but Evia, have you thought about putting together an actual Ezine where people can get the blog postings sent to them in an email?*

Sorry I didn't respond sooner to this. Yes, I've thought about it but so many other projects jump to the top of the list. ☺ Maybe one day.

Tue Aug 12, 03:48:00 PM EDT

Deidre said...

> *People were looking for seats, yet these women sat at separate tables talking in blaring voices to each other.*

That's one of the things that I hope I don't do. When I talk, I tend to be loud sometimes. Not in the uncouth, ugly sense. Not all of the time. Usually, it depends on if I'm interested in a subject. I have no idea I'm talking loudly until a friend says, "Shh, you're being loud," etc. Plus, it depends on where I am or when I get comfortable where I am. What do I do to work on this?

Tue Aug 12, 03:56:00 PM EDT

Ellant said...

Great post. I understand what the 17-year-old girl is feeling. I think every person has problems with self-esteem. I agree with everyone else. Turn off the TV, don't read the magazines, and just shut yourself off from this beauty-crazed world. You know, I've always been able to find something attractive about someone. I don't believe in *ugly*. Beauty is in everyone. I think there were only two times where I might have thought someone was ugly. Not only were they unattractive, but they also had nasty attitudes.

I can't stand Tyra. I don't like her show. I don't like the fact that she dresses up for a day and then goes back to her mansion. I don't think dress-up helps the poor. If anybody has the video clip of the black woman saying that she only dated an Asian for her kids to have good hair and lighter skin, please send it to me. I'm thinking about doing a post on the hypocrisy of interracial relationships.

Tue Aug 12, 04:23:00 PM EDT

Evia said...

> *If you go to YouTube, there are countless videos (and comments on these videos) that are made to put down the beauty of black women.... I notice a lot of these videos are made by black American men . . . .*

Yes, this is all the more tragic because it's messing up the heads of many black girls and young bw. I think this is a way for some of the DBRbm to cut bw down, slow bw down, so that the women will be weaker and will therefore remain within their reach. Look at it as an analogy. It's almost the perfect way for predators to keep their prey within reach by poisoning them, verbally—on a constant basis.

I personally have never watched one of those videos and

never will because I have no interest in what DBRbm, in general, are saying. I've already made my assessment of their condition and it's not good, so I'm indifferent to them. However, I think many black girls and bw are looking for a positive sign of some sort, so they keep looking and listening to the DBRs.

However, like a moth drawn to a flame—and gets burned to a crisp by it—many black girls and young bw watch those videos and some are permanently scarred because they have no mental protection. I think that eventually, there will be lawsuits filed against *YouTube* about putting up harmful material like that.

An aside, the 17 year-old young bw sent me the following note last night:

Thank you for taking the time to respond to my email. I really appreciate it. I also appreciate what people said in their comments.

I do have self-image problems. I don't think they are self-esteem problems. I mean, I feel good about my personality but I think it is my looks that get me down. I have been thru a lot when I was little. And I hope you don't mind if I email you now and then because you make me feel comfortable talking to you about myself.

In school, I come off as this 'loud, know-what-she-wants' type of person. And I feel that I play into this role even if that is not who I really am. I find it hard to break out of myself because there is this image that a lot of people have of bw/bg and it is not easy to break out of, because you are scared of what some people in the black community think of you. I haven't found the balance between me and the color of my skin.

Thanks for listening.

I'm {{{HUGGING YOU}}}! You are *not* alone. Never feel that you are. You're so beautiful! So real! Your beauty radiates through cyberspace to us all. I know there are many young men who are looking for a *real* young women like you instead of all the fake ones out there and I know they'd love to meet you and get to know you. You are rare and special.

Please *know* that we're all here for you. Many bw have experienced some of what you're going through in some way, so we understand. We're with you in spirit and wish we could be with you to support you there. Instead, we connect with you here and are happy to do so. You are our little sister.

You're so brave for speaking out about the role you feel you must play. Tens and hundreds of thousands of young bw like you are oppressed by that same destructive role, playing that same role that the bc loves for bw to play, "acting" like a bw, like a caricature of a loud, coarse, sapphire, strong *sistagirl*. That's why some of us talk about it so much here.

One of these days, when enough bw wake up and begin to promote and protect their own interests, no bw will feel the need to play a role that harms her.

Until then, please try to stop playing the role little by little each day because you are losing your beautiful, *authentic* self in the process. You must never lose or forget who *you* are because *you* are unique. There's only one of you in the world and I don't even want to imagine the loss of the *authentic you*.

Please be determined to move away from people who you feel you have to play a role around. Know that there are many people who you can be around who won't require you to play a role.

You may not be able to break away totally now, but promise me that you will start planning it now and put your plan into action little by little, so that you will be free one day soon.

Please stay connected to us. You are in our hearts and prayers.

Tue Aug 12, 04:41:00 PM EDT

Anonymous said...

Evia, I stay as far away as I can from the ABCs (Acting Black Crew). When there are certain events in my city where I know they will be in attendance, I will not go because you cannot enjoy yourself. They are usually extremely obnoxious, disrespectful, and the language is atrocious. And if I have to constantly ask someone to refrain from the profanity, it is guaranteed to become violent. So I'd rather not be in their midst. You don't have to worry about them attending a cultural event because it's too *white* for them.

I've gone to various events and sat among the whites there. My family and I would probably be the only family of color at the beginning of the event, and then here comes the abcs to sit right by us and act as if we know them. Most of the time, once they start, we'll get up and move because I am trying to enjoy a show. You cannot enjoy yourself at a movie or any public place— if they're there—because of their ignorance.

The best way for any women to survive and come into her own is to not define herself through others. Each of us is the author of our own 'book' and only we *should* be the authors of own book.

In this country, I find it so hypocritical that many people are taught to believe in God. Yet at the same time, they are told to believe in the thoughts, comments, ideas, and perceptions of what others have of you, as being the most important. No wonder why so many men and women suffer from such low self-esteem.

The media has a vast responsibility of disseminating information to the masses. Rarely do they communicate positive and inspiring communication to the masses. Many people solely depend on them to communicate this information; that is why so many people believe everything that is told to them by the media without doing the research themselves. The biggest way to solve this dilemma is to read and find out the truth for yourselves and know who you are and never let others define you.

Honor and love yourself and never deal with anyone who cannot honor you. Believe in the *actions* of others. If someone merely says that they love you, always ask yourself: "Are they *showing* love to me?" Too many women fall due to this fatal mistake and never pay attention to how someone treats them. It's no lie that when someone says, *'Actions speak louder than words.'*

The actions of BM are *showing* us that many of them do not want us. Obviously, many of them believe we are not worthy of living well, which is the biggest lie ever told. You will live well when you stay away from men who are damaged goods and want to bring you down to their level. Hurting people, hurt other people.

Every woman deserves the best that this planet has to offer.

It ought not be denied to anyone because of one's skin tone. So if anyone thinks that you are not entitled to the good life, think again. You are of this world's humanity and what ever was given to humanity belongs to all of us and not afforded to only a few. My belief is that I am as privileged as the next person and I will not be denied, and neither should anyone else.

Tue Aug 12, 04:45:00 PM EDT

Yvette said...

> *Very few people in this society are going to accept any kind of sad sob story from an AA female. That was one of the first lessons I learned as a girl.*

AMEN! AMEN! AMEN! AMEN! AMEN! AMEN! & AMEN!

And those black women who don't get that, God bless you. I bet that the "Black in America" documentary made a lot of people think that the poor black woman has no hope.

But what they fail to realize is that black women have evolved quite a bit and are still evolving. A lot of us are (to take your words, Evia: *"Living Well"*!

Evia, I have friends that are dating and marrying white men who *treat* them well. We can see this in their faces and in their lives. And we do look. ☺ These same women would have never considered doing this before. Every girlfriend that I have has a girlfriend who is marrying or dating a white guy of good standing. That was unheard of just 5 to 10 years ago. I mean totally.

So, bw are definitely getting away from the *"only a brother"* mentality. And the best thing about it is that my girlfriends who are dating/marrying white guys never sit around and say anything bad about black men. They just don't look back.

Tue Aug 12, 09:31:00 PM EDT

Yvette said...re:

> It's only a hair "style" to them, which can be changed. Our "worth" is not connected with our hair to them—the way it is with many bm.

If you saw the movie *Something New*, you would have seen how the black man loved Sanaa Latham's long, flowing weave and the white man wanted her to wear her natural hair.

> . . . this type of fixation on hair and complexion comes mainly from certain elements of AAs these days. If you're not around them much, you don't experience it. So not all AAs are fixated on or traumatized by hair and complexion issues. Not saying that many blacks don't think about it, but it seems that certain elements of black folks have almost made hair and skin shade a religion or at the very least, a **mania.**

That's true. I am dark-skinned and I never experienced dark-skinned prejudice in my family. We are high-yellow to dark black and we are very, very close-knit. White racists are not prejudiced against dark skinned people. They are prejudice against *all* black people.

> At any rate, at one point soon, wm and bw will both learn the necessary steps and there will be an explosion of bw-wm/bw-nonbm relationships and marriages. I'm a bw. I know bw. Bw are very resourceful. Throughout history, bw have always found a way. They will find a way in this case too because many wm, like yourself, are also ready and eager to do their part. That's the key: the man has to be willing to do his part. So, it's only a matter of time before the dam breaks.

I think there already is somewhat of an explosion of wm/bw relationships.

Regarding "acting black," instead of saying 'acting black,' I would say: *acting ignorant and uncouth*. Being black is not synonymous with that.

Tue Aug 12, 10:13:00 PM EDT

Phenombw said...re:

> *I remember when I was younger; I had a problem with the way I looked. My hair wasn't long enough, I wasn't flirty enough, wasn't light enough, and wasn't showing off my body enough. And one day I said f**k it! I turned off the TV (BET/MTV), turned off the radio (it's been almost 4 years since I tuned into the radio), stopped buying magazines that said "do this and that to get the man you want," and you know what? I built up my own self-esteem. . . And people took notice.*

☺ Adelia, you are a trip! I can understand that it can be best to turn off/stop reading/stop looking at everything. But, what I find myself wondering especially for the teen and young bw is how to get them to combat it when it's right in their faces and all around them everyday. How to get them to not be touched even a bit?

This is what I question. I think turning off everything is good, but could it be good only temporarily? I wish we could come up with a plan to get these younger bw to not be affected with the *"you're not beautiful because you're black"* blows, without them having to stop watching TV or reading magazines, which more than likely will not represent themselves. We need to let them know that it's okay to not see a reflection of themselves in the media continuously, because the good stuff is never easily and or readily revealed or shown off. I think that's when the 'my beauty is untouchable' mindset will be conquered. I know for myself anytime I come across a younger bw, I make it a mission to let her know how beautiful and unique she is.

I sense that since I'm still young not to far above them in my mid 20's and the way I carry myself, it makes them look up to me immediately. You'd better believe I use it to my advantage to pass the torch.

This brings me to when I drove 3 hours away to go visit my brother, my niece, her mom, and the rest of their family for the 4th of July. My niece, who is 12 and really beautiful, with gorgeous light brown eyes. I can remember me and my brother and others having a conversation with her about self-respect. The guys were talking more about *pimp crap,* because they were drunk. Btw, I started the self-respect conversation with her and then everyone else had to put their 2 cents in. She was listening and paying more attention to what I had to say. One reason is because she hasn't seen her auntie in years, so I grabbed her hands pleading to her to not ever let men abuse her emotionally or physically, and to not restrict herself to only bm when she started dating.

When I said that, the whole room got silent, including my brother—with anger. It was like everyone tried to throw this piece and that piece out at me, but when I threw mine's out, it got silent. So I was able to dramatize it a bit more. Lol! I'm counting on her to never forget what I told her, due to how it went down. Their silence and evil stares were not stopping my words of wisdom.

The strange part was when I told her to not just date bm when she starts dating, she started to look down and somewhat ashamed. It may be because everyone was eyeballing the heaven out of her to see her reaction. My brother then tried to do the Dbrbm sneak attack and said he teaches her about boys and he deals with white people but not like that, because (drum roll— here we go y'all—let's say it together loud): "They are *all* racist."

She wanted to see more of what I was about to say to the point that when I was getting ready to drive back home, she was begging me to stay and thinking up of all kinds of thing to stop me from getting on the road. I told her mom to make sure she keeps in touch with me so I can spend time with my niece. Do you think anyone has called me yet? No. But that's alright, because the next time I'm in her city, I will be taking advantage of some alone time with my niece.

Tue Aug 12, 10:16:00 PM EDT

Wanda said...

"pimp crap" around a 12 year old? Wow!

Tue Aug 12, 11:18:00 PM EDT

Hsa said...

Phenombw, thank God for women like you, who have stepped up to enable your niece to 'live well.' God bless you.

I wish I had a stronger plan to rescue all those precious black girls, knowing that they must be going through hell, what with the 'Yung Bergs' (with his: *"I don't do dark meat"* poisonous statements and the like) that populate their environs. The confusion and fear must be overwhelming. It makes me feel very powerless at times.

I am seriously thinking of focusing only on our black girls, our precious young ones. We oldies have had our chance, I tell ya!

Supposing I wanted to Date a White Guy...? [website]

Berona said... @ PhenomBW..

That is good girl...gettin' em' while they are *young*!

Wed Aug 13, 07:18:00 PM EDT

Anonymous said...

You know, there is something I noticed a while back in African movies—*Nollywood* (Nigerian made movies). I notice the hairstyles of the women, especially the weaves. I've also been watching Haitian movies. Anyway, you will have women who have natural hair one day, a blowout style the next, back to natural the next, a wig or weave the next. It's like they don't really care. It's just a style. Anyway, I don't know if women there still think like this as they are perming like crazy just like we are. I just think that this is a cool way to think. Do what you want with your hair as long as you are keeping it healthy.

You can have it natural and do whatever the hell you want, or you can perm either way it's up to you. Plus we can change whenever or whatever we want to. That's why brothas get mad at black women. We can change.

Wed Aug 13, 11:07:00 PM EDT

Art said...

> *.. when I was getting ready to drive back home, she was begging me to stay.*

In my case, it was putting my bi-racial granddaughter on a plane for home last Saturday. But it was the same kind of thing.

She just clung to me, wanting to stay. I think it's the vision of safety, calm, and happy life that opens up before their eyes. Broke my heart.

But I talked to my daughter-in-law and we're working out a plan for her to come out at Christmas and stay with me for half the next year. We're just going to have to stiffen up until then. But we can call each other, and I can send her things.

Yvette said...

> *You know there is something I noticed about African movies . . . Do what you want with your hair as long as you are keeping it healthy.*

You also see a lot of bw wearing natural hair styles in NYC. It depends on the region.

Thu Aug 14, 10:22:00 AM EDT

Lavette said...

Hi Evia, I was a subscriber of your then Gen II blog and loved it just as much as I love this one too.

I found out about this blog from a friend, and I must say I've learned so much from it. It confirmed what I've been feeling and thinking for a long time now. I never bought into the notion that black women's beauty was *less than* anybody else's. I've never believed that the Good Lord put all the special qualities into white women only and then left us out, but if you listen to these DBRs, they will certainly have you thinking that there is so much wrong with black women.

When the truth is we are just fabulous! So please continue your good work because we need to hear this information and we are listening. I know I am.

Thu Aug 14, 11:28:00 AM EDT

Tess said...

Evia, thanks again for your work to help bw see the light. My concern is that bw who have the *'nothin but a bm'* mentality are not going to come to this blog in the 1st place. Do you think you can create a blog about bw and any other topic, such as black woman celebrities and make sure you start to slowly put in the blog your ideas about bw dating out? I would do it but I'm not as good with words as you are. ☺ Thanks!!

Fri Aug 15, 06:41:00 AM EDT

Sherry said...

> *Do you think you can create a blog about bw and any other topic, such as black woman celebrities and make sure you start to slowly put in the blog your ideas about bw dating out?*

Hey Tess, while I am not Evia's spokesperson or anything—lol—I really think she does *more* than enough. I think she has about 4 different blogs going right now.

The truth is, some BW are not ready (and many never will be) to hear anything different. They are just uncomfortable being anywhere outside of the BC (whatever that is to them).

Maybe *you* should start the blog you suggested for Evia to start and then you can control slowly (or quickly) how you want it to unfold. I really think the work Evia does here is a lot, to begin with. It is not easy running *one* blog on a daily basis; Evia has 4 already, and 4 is more than enough.

Side Note: Although I am certainly not (and never was) a BW entrenched in DBRbm's foolishness, I did find this website purely by accident because I was looking for writings about BW/WM, or just IR with BW as the focus, in general, and I came across this site ('seek and ye shall find' literally). Same with Sara's bw-nonbm's site. I discovered hers independently of this one. These are the kind of sites you have to actually be actively looking for, so it always surprises me when I see trolls. If they are in such disagreement, why on earth are they actively looking for and patrolling these kinds of sites?

Fri Aug 15, 05:52:00 PM EDT

Anonymous Male said...

It does seem the media does perpetuate this mentality that white is more attractive than black or lighter is more desirable than darker. If you don't realize it, I will say this: it is total and absolute BS.

Take for instance, Gabrielle Union. She is black and not a lighter complexioned woman, and would anyone say she is not attractive and desirable. I didn't think so. She is a very, very, very beautiful woman. She could probably reform the most stubborn KKK member. Any man would give his soul to hold her in his arms, run his hand through her black hair, and look into those lovely dark candy eyes.

Nichelle Nichols is a darker BW. Lt. Uhura was the sexpot of the starship *Enterprise*. She was responsible for giving many of us geeky white boys the *fevah*.

What about the late RnB singer, *Aaliyah*? This young woman had looks, brains, talent, and class. She was the queen of female singers. This woman was sex appeal incarnate. I balled my eyes out, when she died, and I don't feel for celebrities as a general rule.

So, I hope this gives some evidence that black or darker is not less attractive or less desirable than white or lighter. Dark is desirable, Alalam almeen, ammen.

(*always and forever, so be it,* in Aramaic)

2

Talk Openly, Honestly with White/Non-Black Partner about Race—Part 1

July 11, 2006

By the time a black woman is in a serious relationship with a white or other non-black man, they should have had talks about racial issues to the extent that they've covered all the potential racial land mines to the satisfaction of them both. However, depending on the social exposure level, maturity, intellectual adventurousness, and other key factors, some couples do not need to discuss these issues much at all. If either partner has emotional stumbling blocks in discussing any aspect of race, I would consider this a red flag. It cannot be ignored.

Some people think that if you date or marry a white mate, you can't be fully relaxed when talking about race and racial issues with your white partner or even in the vicinity of whites. Other people, of course, think that when a black person has a white partner, it indicates that the black person *has 'forgotten where they came from'* or is trying to *escape* being black. These are stereotypes but as the saying goes 'stereotypes have at least a kernel of truth' *some* of the time and for *certain* people. Such is the case with the situation of some blacks hesitating to talk about racial issues with their white mates.

Let me stress here that this is a non-issue in some cases since many white male spouses of black women have a well-developed social consciousness about racial issues in America and therefore don't shrink from such discussions.

The level of comfort in talking about race or racial issues with any white or black person—male or female—depends on the individual's makeup, their personal conflicts about racial issues (if any), the strength and texture of the person's racial/ethnic *identity*, etc. Some black women, for instance, have white girlfriends with whom they never talk openly and honestly about race. I've also heard (don't know how true this is) that some black-white interracial couples steer clear of discussing racial issues altogether.

I watched a video the other day where a black man flatly stated that he could never have a committed relationship with a white woman because he wouldn't be able to share the everyday racial experiences he has and expect her to understand his feelings about them. He felt that *only* another black person could relate.

This is a stereotype because there are many black people who cannot relate the experiences of other black people these days. Many blacks simply do not have enough common experiences. At the same time, there are some white people who can relate very well to black peoples' experiences. And selecting a mate is all about vetting carefully to find a compatible mate.

If people were this incapable of empathy and relating to experiences beyond their own, most women and men would never connect because many men can never experience life as a woman. Thus, they wouldn't be able to meet a woman's emotional needs, and the converse is also true. I think that the disconnect between virtually *any* woman and man is even broader than between a caring white husband when it comes to understanding a traumatic racial experience of his black wife. This has proven to be my situation more than once. So I know this is true. If it's true in my case, I know it can be true in many other cases. Likewise, I'm sure that some white partners cannot relate.

When I began dating white men, I could tell by some of the politically-correct comments that some made about race, their awkward reactions, or their silence that they were uncomfortable with the topic. I'd sit there wondering, "Now what am I doing sitting here with a man who can't talk openly about race or racial issues?" When I probed, one guy said he didn't want to make *me* uncomfortable. ☺ I pointed out that I'm never uncomfortable discussing race, so he was projecting his own discomfort onto me.

I wouldn't even want to be with a black man who doesn't want to discuss racial issue if discussing race is pertinent to understanding a situation better. Some black men are like that.

After all, race is a major issue in a black person's life, and it's always a front burner issue if you live in the U.S., so why should one *avoid* talking about it, when it's relevant?

I'm also the type of person who likes to talk about just about everything in a no-holds barred but tactful fashion, especially with those who are close to me, so I wanted a man who could *go there* with me because talking and sharing are major aspects of good companionship to me.

Anyway, along came my husband who is a voracious reader, well educated, well traveled, has an awesome intellect, and therefore has a profound life of the mind. He never ceases to amaze me with his range of knowledge. When I brought up the topic of race on our first date, he had no problem discussing it. Later, I found out one of the reasons why. My white husband doesn't consider himself to be "white"—*in the usual sense.*

Posted by Evia at 7/11/2006 12:43:00 PM

3

Talk Openly and Honestly with White/Non-Black Partner about Race—Part II

July 12, 2006

To the bw who responded to my post yesterday by contacting me personally, thanks for your e-mail and the encouragement. In this post, I will follow up on yesterday's post and will respond to your note, since I was going to swerve in that direction anyway.

The bw I'm referring to here said she has a white boyfriend who feels that black women with white men are "settling" for white guys and are only with them because we can't get a good black man. She said she tries to assure him that she can find good black men, but they are not as good for her as he is. Apparently, this is an ongoing source of friction for them—a terrible feeling for him to have, and it certainly sounds like an unpleasant situation for her.

She pointed out in her e-mail to me that black women and black men who are in IR relationships tend to position their argument for being in IRs in this manner. In other words, many blacks seem to feel the need to *justify* why we date and marry out of the race and give the impression on some level that it's because we couldn't find suitable black mates.

Yes, I think both black men and black women sometimes make the claim to an extent that we're with others because we couldn't find black people who were as suitable and compatible. On the other hand, *some* blacks who date or marry interracially do not feel free to reveal *all* the reasons they're with a white mate, or in some cases, the main reasons. They know that others will judge them as self-haters, call them traitors to their race, say they're infected with internalized racism (which associates whites with all things "positive"), or accuse them of having a white fetish.

For instance, a couple of weeks ago, a bw I know who is married to a white guy told me that she loves blue-eyed men and said that's one of the reasons she was strongly attracted to her blue-eyed husband. Is that a fetish? I thought a bit about that. Is that different than a black man saying he is strongly attracted to straight hair and prefers blonds.

Or what if a man says he prefers a woman with a large derriere or large breasts. Men make these comments openly and quite often. Both of these male preferences are perfectly acceptable to say, so *if* the bw's preference for blue-eyed men is a fetish, then don't these males also have fetishes? I'd say, definitely.

In both cases, objectifying is taking place—but the bw who likes blue eyes would be pounced on (at least, by other blacks) whereas the guys might be patted on the back by other men for objectifying big breasts (large mammary glands) and big butts (excess fat tissue in the buttocks). This is just something to think about.

But I digress, so back to the main topic of talking openly with a white mate.

It was a downer for my husband when I told him a couple of times at the beginning of our relationship that due to the racial polarization in the U.S. and other people projecting their issues onto our togetherness, it would be easier if he were darker or *black*. It was my way of saying that I wished we lived in a country where the racism virus wasn't on the rampage.

Call me insensitive, but I did that a couple of times before he told me angrily one day, "Stop it. I can never change my skin shade, and you know it!" I apologized and never said anything like that to him again. I think I thought that as a white man—with the whole world *supposedly* at his disposal—he could take it. What's a little thing like his wife preferring for him to be darker? ☺ This did not mean I preferred to be with a black man.

But why did I say it in the first place? How would I have felt if he'd told me he wished I were a white woman? Most definitely, I wouldn't have looked at it the way he did at all because as a white man, and as a man, he had the male privilege to ask a white woman or any woman to be his wife.

To connect this to the anxiety felt by the white husband of my note writer, I've often pointed out that if **prior** to meeting

Darren, I'd met an AA man or **any** other type of quality, loving, lovable, suitable and compatible man who loved me *and had Darren's qualities and traits (or similar ones),* and if that guy had asked me to marry him, as Darren did, I would have most likely married him. After all, I'd already married once to a non-AA man. Marrying a man within my racial or ethnic group for the mere/main reason that we share the same ethnic group defies common sense to me. Unfortunately, many AA women do this for this sole reason, and many of them live to regret it.

Some people believe a bw has settled for a white man because when you consider the social difficulties some bw still face for dating and marrying a wm, people wonder why would she do it if she had a choice. The fact is that, prior to recently, many AA women never knew white men were on their dating and marriage *menu.* ☺ It's like a woman only seeing chicken noodle soup on the local restaurant's menu, and then one day the restaurant starts serving gazpacho soup. If she orders gazpacho and likes it, is she *settling* for it? Not at all.

For me, it's *always* been a matter of the man's qualities and traits, his compatibility with me, his love for me, my love for him, and his desire and request to share his life with mine, within the bounds of matrimony. That's about it.

Whew! This is exactly what I mean about trying to just live and breathe in racially plagued America. Everything pertaining to race is put under a microscope and virtually always looks diseased and ugly. That's what I meant when I said to Darren that it would have just been easier if he'd been black. However, I showed by marrying him that I wasn't about to miss being with him because of other peoples' issues.

I realize now that I was just being dense to an extent with my *politically incorrect* statement to him, but it also showed my level of comfort with him, even at that early point. I knew he was *white*, but I didn't *feel* I was talking to a "white" guy. Also, I wanted him to get used to my 'stream of consciousness' comments about things and get comfortable with the real me, even when I might say stupid stuff. I wasn't going to walk on eggshells around him or "be careful" and I didn't want him to 'be careful' with me. UGH! *Being careful* constantly with your mate can cause deep resentment and put an abnormal strain on a relationship.

That's one thing that interracial couples just have to learn to reject: *other peoples' issues.* If you allow other people to put *their* issues about your relationship on you, they will do it. This is because most black and white people in the U.S. are full of issues about race and have absolutely no opportunities to work through them. Race is still a mostly hush-hush affair. Progressive white people are still not supposed to talk about it or feel they're expected to be "color-blind," as if seeing a black person as *black* is a bad thing. Many blacks find it discomfiting that whites try to be *color-blind.*

Therefore, many blacks and whites will do practically anything to avoid discussing the topic with each other. Mostly, white and black adults resort to avoiding each other—unless forced to mingle with each other at work or at school.

Anyway, I recall asking Darren at that time, whether he ever wished I were white, and he asked with incredulity on his face, "Why would I be with you if I preferred to be with a white woman?" And with the answer implied in his question, he was asking, "Do you think I 'settled' for you?" He had a good point. He's an attractive white man of high educational level and comfortable means. He could be with virtually any race of woman he chooses. He didn't have to *settle*.

He also doesn't care about social ease and feels that having the woman of his choice is his prerogative. He believes that people who harbor racist notions *"need to work on themselves."*

And it really is a different situation for whites. The social dynamics are vastly different. Whereas many whites have learned to be ashamed of their racism or not to voice racist sentiments or couch them in politically correct ways, many non-critically-thinking AAs—unable to recognize and resolve the fact that they have internalized many racist beliefs about themselves or unable to exorcise these beliefs—derive a sense of power and pride in their blackness by acting out their prejudice towards whites.

This is how the whole "acting black" phenomenon got started where blacks pattern their behavior after caricatures and stereotypes of black behavior. They believe that being *pro*-black means being anti-white and when it comes to interracial relationships, some blacks—through the pro-black lens—believe that the *only* reason a black person dates or marries a white person is due to their deep-seated need to reject their black/African heritage. These are some of the blacks that some interracially married black women must contend with regularly because many people in the black community, especially, feel comfortable attacking bw for our choices in all aspects of our lives.

My husband, Darren, on the other hand, feels that he can

be with whomever he pleases and how dare anyone question his choice. I feel the same way internally, but I'm not accustomed to not being questioned about my choices. I don't allow anyone to prevent me from making the best choices for me, but I don't have the power he has to prevent others from trying to interfere with my choices by questioning me.

Whereas he would never allow anyone to question him about why he married me, black people question me—directly and indirectly—with some black men claiming that I and other black women like me have "betrayed" them or are "sellouts." I've had some people question my sanity. Or some bm try to lessen their feelings of rejection by minimizing a loving relationship between a bw and a wm. They claim that a bw would only want a wm for the wm's *supposed money,* or because she couldn't get a "brotha." Many deep-seated issues of insecurity in some bm become full-blown and sometimes out of control when they see bw in loving relationships with wm. This is why bw are verbally attacked or sometimes even physically when bm—many of whom date or are married to ww—see a bw with a wm.

Of course, I realize that such accusations of bw "betraying bm" are an attempt to *control* black women's sexuality and keep us *'in our place.'* However, such accusations as these are reasons why *some* black women feel they need to have a ready explanation or justification for why they date or marry outside the race.

This is just how warped and issue-ridden some AAs are about bw-wm relationships. Fortunately, this is a minority of AAs. I've also had some older bw and bm surprisingly, *congratulate* me on marrying a wm. They explained that for so long, sexual mingling between bw and wm could not result in marriage due to the illegality of it, so they now consider it an achievement or sign of major progress. ☺

Anyway, after a year or so in the relationship, I discovered that I wasn't even aware of Darren's "white"ness anymore because after all, "white" is simply a political label. You can't have a satisfying relationship if you allow politics to be the third partner in a relationship. I'm aware of the politics of his skin shade sometimes, but it's totally insignificant when we interact with each other.

The only time I'm aware of his skin shade now is when we're out in public and someone looks at us oddly or a bit too long. I always conclude that either the person likes what s/he sees, or they're struggling with their own issues. If the latter is the case, I always hope they win the struggle.

Posted by Evia at 7/12/2006 03:30:00 PM

4

Can a White Man Love a Black Woman?

July 25, 2006

My post today is a response to comments Angie made about my post yesterday where I asked, "Why do people ask us how we met?" I think what Angie said deserves to be addressed in my post today because her comments touched on the reasons why there are so few couples like us. She said the following:

> *I'm in a serious and loving relationship with a black man whom I've known for quite a long time. So, I'm good, but I'm still intrigued by IRs. And I'm not sure why. As a junior in high school, I had a crush on a white guy; well, we had a mutual crush. It didn't go much further because we were both afraid of what our families would think. (My mother did not approve, and I don't think his family would have either).*
> *As an adult, I've only been on one date with*

a white man, living in Ohio. It did not go well, not because he was white, but because he was unsuitable for me. So, after reading your posts and comments, I've begun to wonder why I am co curious about IRs. Is it because I grew up hearing that a white man could not really love a black woman in the same way a black man could? The romantic in me has never wanted to believe that, so maybe I search for instances that disprove what I was taught. Or maybe I'm facing some of my own prejudices, because I'm not sure I could truly love a white man without having some hang-ups about racial stuff. Hmmm, this is something to think about.

Hence, the question, "Where did you two meet?" It's like asking, "Where is that magical place that none of the s#it that we have lived with for so long doesn't exist, and I can feel free to love a man, and not see his skin color as a reminder of emotions and actions that are opposite of love?" Do you understand me?

Angie, thanks for helping me to understand that question better. Wow! That *magical place*. That's a beautiful idea. If I ever do write an interracial romance, which I have thought about doing, may I use that as the title of the book? (smile)

I think many people have a fascination with interracial coupling. I hate to make it sound boring, but the fact is that we are just like you and your guy—a man and a woman in a loving relationship. There are so many stereotypes and myths that black and white people have about each other. I think that you, I, and every other black woman have been told certain things about white men to keep us away from them because of the history. Our folks couldn't protect us from their advances during slavery and afterwards. So most black females were taught to stay away from white men and to *distrust* them, and for good reasons. I received the same training.

Interestingly, I never wondered about whether a white man could love a black woman until you mentioned it. I mean, *why not?* If my husband doesn't really love me, he certainly treats me like he does, and that's good enough for me. ☺

I realized quite some time ago that both whites and blacks were/are being manipulated by the 'powers that be.' I've personally had relationships with several white people (males and females) in my life, who refused to be manipulated by the power structure when it came to racial matters. When my husband came along, he showed me he was that type of man—a strong one, who thinks for himself.

Anyway, before I ever went out with him, I gave some serious thought to his race because his color is associated with a lot of ugliness, insofar as we, blacks, are concerned, but I made a decision *not* to hold his race against him. He didn't do any of those ugly things. Once I took that into account and looked at him, I saw a man, not a race—just a single, solitary man who was letting me know that all he wanted to do was love me and share his life with me.

You asked: "Where is the place . . . where *none* of this s#it exists . . . . ?" Nowhere. Expect the *good* from life, not the bad. Life is not an *all-or-none* situation. You must work on yourself to see each man as an *individual.* Vet or evaluate each man as *one* man, based on how he treats you—an *individual* woman. In general, prejudging people cuts you off from many wonderful experiences. Of course, be careful, but don't prejudge.

However, I don't equate white prejudice with black

prejudice. In many cases, black prejudice is totally justified; in most cases, white prejudice is not. My husband would be the first to agree with me on this. Most often, black prejudice is a matter of safety, self-preservation, whereas white prejudice functions to support selfishness, greed, create more white privilege and protect it.

Re racial hang-ups, we make it a point to talk about stuff like that a lot with each other. See my post from earlier this month: *Talk Openly . . . . about Race.*

Posted by Evia at 7/25/2006 12:17:00 PM

COMMENTS:

Anonymous said...

It won't work, because his family will never, ever accept you. I've been in the exact same situation as you are, and it was three years of hell. There were endless discussions, where I was present and never included, and in many of them, the atmosphere was made to be so stifling, that I'd leave because of the imposing doom n' gloom that was directed at me. Her family made me feel like I was inferior, an interloper, a spy, a loser. And there were endless amounts of putdowns by them.

My family, however, accepted her and treated her with the utmost respect, and even paid for the bulk of her education, which her family pretended never happened. They acted like the 5% paid for by her alcoholic father was the entire tuition fee. So, materialistic examples aside, I'd never go through that sort of life again. It simply isn't worth it.

When we parted, her family threw her a big party, which I

heard about through a dozen answering machine messages left by her drunken brothers and other relatives. There seems to be a serious amount of reverse racism, which most in her family wielded like a gun, a crutch, and a badge to wear. I never have ever spoken to her again, and have returned countless letters and cards, all stamped *'Refused By Addressee'*. I think the guilt got to her after I left, but I'm quite happy now with my new wife, baby, and new home. It was the biggest mistake I ever made when I began the relationship with her.

Tue Jul 25, 01:45:00 PM EDT

Evia said...

Am I right that you are a black man who was in an IR relationship with a white woman? Well, I'm glad you've bounced back. Be cautious. Vet people and situations, but don't prejudge.

I would never be in a relationship with a man whose family didn't treat me well. My husband's family is nice to me. I'm not the sort of person who accepts mistreatment of any sort. I'm not 'big and bad' but I think too highly of myself to allow that.

Tue Jul 25, 03:36:00 PM EDT

Anonymous said...

Nice idea with this site. It's better than most of the rubbish I come across.

Fri Aug 11, 05:58:00 AM EDT

Anonymous said...

You are *excellent*. And so is your site! Keep up the good work. Bookmarked.

Wed Aug 16, 01:15:00 PM EDT

5

Dana and Andrew—A Love Story

March 1, 2008

Evia,

I hope you are well. I have been reading your blog for a while and wanted to share my happiness with you.

My fiancée, Dana, and I met a little over five years ago through a mutual friend of ours. I had a crush on her from the minute I saw her. She's sweet, kind, strong, and very beautiful. Over the next three years, we would run into each other a few times a year, and we began to develop a friendship. Every time I had the opportunity to spend time with her, I was reminded of the reasons I was so interested in her and attracted to her: her smile lights up the room. She always makes me laugh. She has strong family values, and she's genuine. She calls things how she sees them and what you see is really what you get.

Unfortunately, every time we would see each other, either she was dating someone, or I was. Finally, we ended up getting the timing worked out and went out on a date, and from that moment on, our relationship has grown and developed over the past 2+ years. I proposed to her just before Thanksgiving, and fortunately, for me, she accepted. We are currently planning our wedding for early 2009. She has become my best friend, my lover, and soon, my wife. I cannot imagine a life without her.

We are interestingly enough, graced with a very diverse group of friends, and many of our close friends are IR couples: WM/AW (a couple of those), BM/WW, BM/IW (Indian), etc. It's been my experience that love doesn't have boundaries; when you find the right person, things just work. That's not to say that everything is always perfect. Solid and loving relationships take work, commitment, compromise, and communication. I have been very blessed to be surrounded by friends and family that all share strong values and respect, along with an understanding that who you are: your personality, your beliefs, your hopes and dreams, and how you treat people and live your life—make life matter for you. These are truly the most important things.

Thanks for reading.

Andrew

6

Living Well: Magical Thinking Will Not Get You There

June 26, 2008

This *'Living Well'* black woman, speaking Korean in the video, is Leslie Benfield. Leslie's boyfriend is Korean.

[LINK posted on site about Leslie's life and career in Korea.]

I just came from the gym and while I was on the treadmill, I watched one of the monitors that featured a program called *Defying the Odds* about an urban male prep school in Chicago that is apparently successfully educating black male students who were considered at-risk or among the so-called "uneducable." I was happy to hear of their success because it will hopefully mean better lives for them. I like seeing people go *up* in life. I'm not the type of person who likes to see anyone go down because any person's misery affects us all in the by and by.

We're all connected.

However, as I watched the young black men, dressed impeccably in uniforms of navy blazer, white shirt, red ties, and looking studious, I was reminded of recent tidbits of discussions I've overheard, the gist of which amounts to "magical thinking." Some of the black women, I've overheard, believe that since Obama has become the Democratic nominee, that will motivate many more black men to become more motivated and more productive and as they become more productive and more successful, more and more of them will run, not walk, to get "back home" to a black woman. These women believe that as black men rise, they're going to pull black women along. ☺

Whereas, the *fact* is that, if we look at what has already occurred, "rising" black men have been a windfall to many *non*-black women. A large percentage of black male doctors, lawyers, business execs, successful business owners, and well-educated/better positioned other American black men date, marry, or marry nonblack women. Many of these men may date and have sex with black women, but if and when they marry, they are more than likely to marry a non-black woman *these days*. I'm talking about the younger set of bm, those under 40.

Marrying or hooking up with a rising or successful bm is probably one of the easiest and quickest ways for a non-black woman to instantly gain several steps up the status, influence, and wealth ladder. Also, a typical non-black woman who goes this route has relatively a lot *less* competition for a "rising" or successful black man than she does for his white male counterpart because the nonblack woman is viewed by many black men as a "premium" woman. This makes it a lot easier for her to secure him or marry him.

For ex., Mrs. Tiger Woods had much less competition for him than she would have had if he had been white. And, I would venture a bet that it was a lot easier for her to get him quickly into a marrying frame of mind than it would have been for *any* black woman.

Because of this, it's a fairly easy feat for a typical non-black woman to marry a rising or prosperous black man if she strategically positions herself in his life. Black women must accept the fact that non-black women are very aware of this option because many rising and prominent black men have let it be known that they and their resources are available to nonblack women. Many of these black men are flatly saying these days that they are seeking nonblack women—*only*. These women see/read proof of this happening everyday, and most rising young black men see other black men doing this.

This is why I know that these "rising" young black men—if or when they actually rise (strong educational background, good employment, status, etc.)—will more than likely pull a non-black or lighter-whiter woman along as a mate.

I don't blame non-black women one iota. *"A woman's gotta do what a woman's gotta do."* They're using what they've got to compete for the highest bidder. These women are simply being shrewd. I'd do the same thing if I were them.

This is one reason why I spend so much time trying to get black women to think and act more shrewdly. Black women have got to put all magical thinking aside and learn how to use their assets to strategically position themselves as "premium" women to the men in the global village who prefer or desire us and are willing to treat us that way—with the emphasis on the "treatment" part. Some men *do* prefer and desire black women or are extremely receptive to committing to a black woman.

To Black women: wishing and hoping that typical black men will view you as a premium woman is simply *magical thinking*. I know that some black men are exceptions in this regard. *Some* do view and treat black women as premium, but exceptions don't make rules.

I realize that many American black women are so worn down and disappointed that they cannot fathom that black women can be viewed and treated as premium women by any man. If you're a black woman who thinks that way, you think that way because you're trapped in a reality that has told you repeatedly that you're somehow *less-than* other women.

I don't share your reality and this is why I can say and stand by all of these infuriating (to some) things that I say and do on my blogsite. ☺ I have never been in that type of 'worn-down' reality, and neither do I think any black woman should be. She certainly ought to *never* cooperate in remaining there. I have never been the 'used and abused' in a relationship with a man because I have *chosen* not to be. *The quality of your life depends on your choices* [subtitle of my BOOK 2], and we all make those choices from moment to moment.

So, in general, these thoughts about a general pattern of rising bm pulling up bw amount to lots of *magical thinking*. This is not what's generally happening. Some AA women are desperately choosing to think that way. Magical thinking occurs when a person thinks, without any/sufficient basis in evidence or reality and without doing anything to make it happen, that a thing is going to occur just because they think or hope it will. I've noticed that a lot of AA women engage in magical thinking when it comes to black men.

Living Well cannot be reached by magical thinking.

Let's jump to the evidence about this. If you read a variety of black American literature and black history, you will quickly realize that the more prosperous, more educated AA men and those bm with more choices in this society have *always*, as a pattern, chosen lighter, brighter, whiter mates. I'm sure I don't need to mention names of prominent black men who did this throughout history and presently. There have been many exceptions, of course, but the world is governed by patterns or what is most likely to occur. The current increasing number of black men who exclusively date, cohabit with, and marry non-black women is not surprising, in view of history. This is an old pattern. American black men have always leaped for lighter, whiter women whenever they could due to internalized racism which says that *'light is good; dark is bad.'*

Yes, some black men do mate and marry darker women, but what percentage of these men are among the more prosperous, most educated, better-positioned, most resourceful black men in any community or region of this country?

Naturally, many black men will argue that a man can't help who he prefers. ☺ It's not that he can't help it; it's that *he doesn't want to change.*

Yet, when these same black men need or have needed help, support, defense, and protection, they drop that preference and become very inclusive towards soliciting help from *all* bw at that point—LOL! Only then do they recognize the value of less-light black women. But here's my question: Why in the world do the excluded and rejected bw keep helping and defending men who have excluded them? I dunno. This is a mystery to a woman like me. I don't love or support anybody who doesn't *treat* me like they love and support me. It's about the treatment, *not* talk.

Black women, please don't set yourselves, your daughters, and other black women you love up for crushing disappointment—again. Don't do that to them. Can the masses of American black women withstand another massive blow?

Any time I'm in the midst of a group of AA women, I hear the bewilderment in their voices and see it on their faces. And when they talk about black men and black women, this is what they talk about. They feel betrayed by "our" rising or successful black men—most of whom have made it patently clear that they don't plan to pull a typical looking or darker black woman *up* and are just not even concerned about bw's betterment.

Let me remind those magical thinking bw that black women de-prioritized their interests during the Civil Rights movement to boost "our" black men who repeatedly hammered the point to black women that we must first all work together to demolish racism. They said: "Only then should a black woman give a blip about any of that sexism mumbo-jumbo."

Many black women worked feverishly—went on the offense and defense for "our" black men. They taught their daughters and other black women to become sista soldiers and shemales— to assert, promote, and defend the interests of "our" black men. Fast forward to the present, this campaign by black women has enabled many of "our" black men to move into a more comfortable position in this society where *some* of them now spit on black women. While they engage in all kinds of defiling behavior against bw, other black men (the "good" brothas) stand by silently or mumble that it's the bw's fault.

Many of these women continue to believe the lies of men who continue to dupe them. What is wrong with a woman's reasoning ability when she believes the *same* lies from the same men over and over? I had a cousin like this. I sometimes thought she'd been cursed. LOL!

The overall behavior pattern of black men has gotten much worse. Even the bm who don't show outright disdain for bw show absolutely no concern for the welfare of bw. Yet, still a large percentage of black women believe that if a black man can *move on up* in this society, he is going to pull a bw with him. SMH! Magical thinking. Yes, he may take a so-called *black* woman, but if he does, there's a very high probability that she's going to look more like Mariah Carey. Just notice the lesser melanin content in the skin shades of the overwhelming most of black wives of prominent black men.

Let me point out once more that these lighter and whiter women are *not* to be blamed for this. It is cowardly for darker black women to *hate on* lighter or whiter women and leave the black men who discriminated—unscathed. These women, as a group, have not done anything to darker women. They can't help it if black men drool over them.

Bw, find your quality man in the global village and *forget* about men who don't regard you as lovable or premium. Stop caring about what black men in general are doing and stop supporting *anyone* who's not supporting you or your interests.

It makes me so happy when I hear from black women who are growing in every aspect of their lives, dating all kinds of quality men, and are determined to move towards the goal of '*Living Well*' in all aspects of their lives.

I bring up this topic of magical thinking here because I seriously don't want bw to be duped again, and I can see this coming with some segments of bw. Remember that bm don't *own* you and you don't own them and more important is that you don't owe them anything that they don't owe you. If they're not loyal to you, then don't be loyal to them. Control your emotions. Don't even think about being loyal to any bm who has not shown his support and loyalty to bw. Don't get swept away—*again*—by self-serving, slick-talking bm talking the 'talk.' Remember that when they come knocking at your door—calling you their *queen*, when they want something.

Let me emphasize here that I'm *not* talking about all black men. For ex., I'm not referring to Obama in this regard. If he does nothing else for bw, he has chosen a darker bw as his mate and elevated her on the world stage to the status of "the fairest (most beautiful and desirable) of them all." *All* black women benefit from this. Indirectly, he has done a great, intangible service for American black women, especially. I'm sure he simply looked at his wife as the beautiful, desirable woman that she is, but many highly positioned black men these days don't seem to be able to see the beauty and worth of a black woman who has a darker skin shade.

I know that some people may want to discount this, but the

woman chosen by a prominent or well-positioned man to be his partner and mother for his children sends a *powerful* message far and wide about the beauty and worth of women of her group. Therefore, Obama's choice of mate has provided a tremendous boost to the self-esteem of countless young black girls across America because his wife, Michelle, is a typical looking darker American black woman. She is also smart and feisty. Many of those darker black American girls and women look at her and think to themselves that "Yes, it's possible a successful man out there somewhere may look at me one day and consider me beautiful and worthy of wifehood even if I don't look like Mariah Carey, Beyonce, or Tiger Woods' wife."

And lots of non-black men in this country and around the world are looking at the beautiful and smart Mrs. Obama. They notice everything about her. They love her looks, her spunk, her fitness, her clothes, her femininity. For ex., everyone remembers that purple dress she wore on the night that he won the nomination, but Darren can't get over how gorgeous she looked in an orange dress she wore on some other occasion. ☺ I've never seen her in 'that orange dress,' but that's his favorite dress on her. He also loves her shapely upper arms that she bares in those sleeveless dresses. Hmmmm . . . Maybe I'd better do some upper arm-sculpting at the gym. LOL! Nah—my arms are almost as cute as hers. ☺

My point is that just like my husband has been checking this woman out, many other men like him have been scoping her too. Here's a New York Times ARTICLE re how the Obamas' influence is already causing the re-shaping of the world's view regarding the beauty of black women.

Back to 'magical thinking.' In general, bw, you must stop letting your feelings or delusions *lead* you, and start thinking and acting strategically. Be shrewd. Make sure that you let *any* man know that he must *show* you—on an ongoing basis—how he feels. You've got to clean out the useless clutter in your brain and prune your entire mindset to only have uplifting, productive thoughts.

Toss out all thoughts that don't help you because as an American black woman, you've been conditioned to think in a way that almost entirely helps others—and not yourself. You are known for letting your softhearted feelings lead you. People know that, and *some* will use that to use you. You're predictable. Others can easily manipulate predictable people. Many black men and others in the bc, for sure, know how to play on your feelings and take advantage of you.

Always promote and protect *your* interests 'first and foremost' [subtitle of my BOOK 1] and keep the focus on *Living Well*. Keep that at the top in your mind, and you'll be fine.

Posted by Evia at 6/26/2008 12:18:00 PM

COMMENTS:

Sarafour said...

I enjoyed this. Props.

Thu Jun 26, 01:50:00 PM EDT 🗑

Miss Pin said...

> *Please don't ever associate me in any way with these numerous black coddlers and enablers of the genocide we currently see taking place in the "black community." This is why I*

> *urge those black women who can hear me to either mate out or die out because help is NOT on the way.*

Evia, I took this quote from one of your other essays. I too am hearing BW expressing their *belief* that Obama's success will somehow translate into BM "waking up" and "coming home." This type of thinking is so dangerous and destructive to BW since the BM who I hear talking, are looking at Obama as their "ticket" to make their stock go up. Some of the BM—I have heard discussing this subject—seem to feel that they will be even *more* accepted by non-BW (and their families) if there is a BM sitting in the White House. BW were NOT a consideration in their equation at all.

Thu Jun 26, 02:18:00 PM EDT

Anjelica said...

Evia, what an absolutely *rocking* thread! I agree so wholeheartedly until I cannot tell you. And the point you make about Michelle Obama—that's the main reason I'm voting for Barack Obama. He has already shown me his fitness to be a leader by the *independent* thinking that made him choose Michelle Robinson to become Michelle Obama.

Thu Jun 26, 02:47:00 PM EDT

Evia said...

> *This type of thinking is so dangerous and destructive to BW since the BM who I hear talking, are looking at Obama as their "ticket" to make their stock go up.*

Exactly, Miss Pin, and it's *you* who convinced me with your whole comment to re-open the commenting here. ☺ What you said is so on point!

The irony of bm looking at Obama to boost their *stock* is that the vast majority of the black votes will come from black women. (smh)

Anyway, we really have to share our thoughts and spread the word regarding these issues because lots of bw are oblivious to the reality of what's going on that will directly impact them. I don't think a lot of bw can allow themselves to believe that many bm just don't care about bw and the "community."

I also just think that bw have to hear the reciprocity message over and over until it sinks in. That's a critical message because it'll force each bw to focus more on herself and look more closely at what she's getting in return for what she's giving, no matter who she's dealing with.

Thu Jun 26, 04:45:00 PM EDT

Evia said...

> *And the point you make about Michelle Obama - that's the main reason I'm voting for Barack Obama. He has already shown me his fitness to be a leader by the independent thinking that made him choose Michelle Robinson to become Michelle Obama.*

For sure! If bw were a stock on the stock exchange, our value would have risen sharply as a result of Michelle being a typical looking AA woman. No matter what happens in November, seeing her at that level is a major self-esteem injection for many, many, many American black women and girls. The pride that she has given them has already changed the course of their lives in more ways than we will ever know.

If American black women had more self-esteem, we are

positioned to be premier women in the world. Despite the onslaught from outside the community and inside, and with practically nobody on our side, *'still we rise.'*

Girl! Considering what many bw endure in their lives, I just find it amazing that many of them still manage to get up out of the bed in the morning. I am so proud to belong to this group of women! This is why we've got to do whatever we can to keep on helping each other to get up in the morning—no matter what we have to do and no matter who doesn't like who we choose to love. I tell you—having a good, loving Quality man by your side definitely puts a spring in a woman's step! LOL!

Thu Jun 26, 05:08:00 PM EDT

Evia said...

> *I enjoyed this. Props.*

Thanks, Sarafour.

Anonymous said...

crying tears of joy

I'm so glad to have you back again, Evia. You are awesome!

Thu Jun 26, 06:00:00 PM EDT

Liza said...

You *still* have it! Keep on telling it like it is, and not how black folks (and specifically duped BW) *wish* it to be.

Magical thinking is nonsense and a total waste of precious time. Slowly but surely, more and more bw are hearing this lifesaving message and acting accordingly. I'm seeing it every day with my own two eyes. And what a blessing it is.

Peace to you and happy to see you're continuing to tell it like it is, *unapologetically.*

You truly love black women. If more bw learned to love and respect themselves as much as you do them, they'd be an unstoppable force enjoying happy, successful, stable, and loving relationships.

There are simply far more successful, family-oriented, attractive, non-damaged, non-colorist white (and other) men out there than black. It's a numbers game, and BW *can* learn how to play it to their advantage, instead of losing damn near every time.

Black women simply need to open themselves up to this worthy population instead of concentrating on those damaged men.

One's life is often a reflection of what one concentrates on most. Bw need to be keenly aware of where they're focusing their attention.

Thu Jun 26, 08:26:00 PM EDT

Art said...

Evia! You're back ☺

Thu Jun 26, 08:34:00 PM EDT

Anonymous said...

First time commenting on your blog. Have been reading awhile now, and I must say I so enjoy reading all the posts. I am learning so much to take with me as I venture out on the dating scene. But the first person that came to my mind as I read this post was O.J Simpson. Classic case of a black man getting support from black women when he got in trouble. Still pains me to this day when he got off. And I think his new girlfriend is white.

Thu Jun 26, 09:05:00 PM EDT

Meryl said...

I love Michelle Obama. That is a role model young girls of *all* races can look up to. Too many times in the BC, these girls get conflicting messages. It goes a lil something like this: *"Get some self-esteem, you're worthless. Get some self-esteem, you're worthless. Get some self-esteem, you're worthless."*

Thu Jun 26, 10:29:00 PM EDT

Anonymous said...

What a great article, Evia. This latest entry has really uplifted my spirits because it allows Black women to know that they have other options. They do not have to end up stuck with a sub-par man because of some one-sided racial loyalty. This blog is very important to let Black women know that they should not wait on anyone who doesn't desire them or find them worthy of being a wife. I also love the emphasis on finding a *quality* man. Anyway, much blessings to you for putting the word out there that Black women are beautiful and we deserve to be happy.

Fri Jun 27, 02:56:00 AM EDT

Donnela said...

How odd that while we, as blacks, are basking in the *'I'm proud of a black man'* moment, we are forgetting one crucial element. The main reason I suspect white people are voting for him is despite his color, Obama was raised in a white household. The crucial element is that his experience isn't uniquely a traditional Black experience. He wasn't *coached* every day by black parents about how hard it is to be black and he didn't get to experience (from bm peers) all the negativity they feel about bw.

Just food for thought.

Fri Jun 27, 08:56:00 AM EDT

Donnela said...

Also, I believe this helped him in choosing Michelle as a mate. He just saw a good, educated, beautiful woman who wanted the same things in life he did. Like I said, his upbringing was vastly different than most bm. Not to take away from his accomplishments, but the black community shouldn't try to latch on to this like this will and can magically turn our communities around.

Fri Jun 27, 09:01:00 AM EDT

Diane said...

Welcome back, Evia. It's good to see the ladies and gentlemen (Hey, Art) on here. I stopped my magical thinking and I am reaping the benefits tenfold. This is an exciting time for black women, despite the uphill battle. A spark of new wave activism is taking place that we have never seen before. Have to get back to packing. We're leaving in three weeks. We have no idea how much junk one accumulates until we have to pack up and move.

Fri Jun 27, 10:28:00 AM EDT

Maya said...

Evia, I am a *huge* fan of your blogs. I am happy to see you still writing on here.

Fri Jun 27, 11:35:00 AM EDT

Evia said...

Hey Liza, Art, Maya, and everybody! Glad y'all dropped in.

@ Diane—Gurl! I'm *so* happy for you, but I could tell from your attitude early on that you were going to "escape" and heaven help anyone who tried to stop you. ☺ Congrats! Tell us all about it one of these old days.

I continue to get notes from some other bw and some wm— that they are meeting, mingling, marrying each other, and are loving their lives together without any of the predicted problems of all the naysayers. They have problems just like any other typical couple.

@ Donnela—Yeah I hear ya. Obama wasn't spoon-fed *'de man is trying to keep a bm down'* or raised on a diet of discounting black women's looks or value as he would most likely have been if he had been raised by most blacks, or even if he had mingled with mostly AA black males while growing up.

My husband, Darren wasn't either and he's a white man. Darren said he was simply told to select a "good" woman.

Likewise, my children are raised to select "good" people for friendships and ultimately for marriage. My children know that racism from racist whites and black self-hatred are forms of mental illness that they must be on guard against and repel.

Fri Jun 27, 01:20:00 PM EDT

Art said...

Hey, Diane—eye on the prize, and don't look back. ☺

Fri Jun 27, 01:35:00 PM EDT

Maris said...

This post is brilliant!

God bless Michelle Obama. The simple fact that after she appeared on *THE VIEW* with her Donna Rico's black and white dress, that dress ran out of stock. It proves how much of an impact she has; people watch her every move, follow her lead, they adore her. That's power! Michelle *definitely* makes our stock go up. Non-black men are definitely paying attention, and so do their parents. They won't be mad at him for bringing his "Michelle" home!

Evia, this is my very first time posting here, but I've been reading your posts religiously since I found your blog (recently, like 2 months ago). You are an inspiration!

Spring said...

Evia, I am glad you're back and that your readers can make comments on your wonderful blog again.

Please, don't ever let the naysayers keep you from doing this very important and much needed work. I really admire both you and Hsa for the service you all have been providing on the behalf of black women in the blogosphere, and hopefully your message will go beyond that.

I think there should be rallies and black women with bullhorns shouting, *"We're mad as hell and we're not going to take it anymore,"* for the betterment of black women everywhere in America.☺

As for *magical thinking*, that has never been me because I have never seen black men, in general, as suitable mates for bw or women of any race, for that matter, in whatever position they were in society.

I really like the Obamas. I believe both bw and bm stock will go up together. The same way bm believe they will be more accepted by non-bw, we (bw) will be more accepted by non-bm. As far as, I am concerned that is all that matters.

Black men have never been in my equation and they should no longer be in the equation of most black women.

Fri Jun 27, 03:25:00 PM EDT

Adelia said...

Hey Evia, I have been reading your recent post and I love it here. I've been going to interracial blogs reading and just being encouraged, so thank you for this blog.

Is there any way I can read your older blogs on this site?

Fri Jun 27, 04:29:00 PM EDT

Julianna said...

Evia, I may not agree with everything you say (so what?), but I love the way you say it and I totally agree with you that all women, including African-American women, must exercise their options in regards to dating/marriage. Otherwise, they will continue to be left behind in the relationship arena.

Black men in my area (I live in Southern Maryland) are dating non-Black women aggressively. I can't go out of my house without seeing at least one BM-WW couple. That's okay with me. I just wish that more Black women would do the same.

What is the sense of being loyal to men who have decided that they don't need to reciprocate?

I'm happily married to a gorgeous Black man (from Haiti and I'm from Jamaica). But I do believe that Black women deny themselves happiness when they don't broaden their choice of men. Further, if you go to England or Canada (where I was born and grew up respectively), you will see loads of Black women with non-Black men. AA women have to join other Black women around the world and stop being lonely and alone!

Keep writing. You have been heavily attacked at some "pro-Black" websites, but I encourage you not to change your message. Your website is refreshing.

Fri Jun 27, 05:58:00 PM EDT

Julianna said...

Evia, I forgot to say that I agree with your comments about Michelle Obama. I really love Barack and his choice of Michelle is one of the many reasons why. I am sure that he had a whole slew of non-black women to choose from, but instead decided on a regular (not light skinned or mixed) Black woman. Go OBAMA!

Fri Jun 27, 06:04:00 PM EDT

Rayda said...

Evia, First of all, I absolutely adore your blog! I have been reading it for about 8 months now. Since I first began my interracial relationship, you have no idea how much you have moved me. So thanks for your support.

I am so happy to be "living well," so kudos to you for reaching out to your sistas, cuz Lord knows who else will.

I assure you many of my friends have looked at my relationship and how my man truly adores and treats me. They are thinking twice about their "magical thinking." This was a great article. I think Michelle Obama is fabulous and Barack is lucky to have her. At U of C, he used to wear a tee shirt that said, "Real Men Marry Lawyers."

So thanks for your article. I missed you.

Fri Jun 27, 07:12:00 PM EDT

Anonymous said...

> *I think there should be rallies and black women with bullhorns shouting, "We're mad as hell and we're not going to take it anymore," for the betterment of black women everywhere in*

America."☺

Evia, can we possibly do this? So many bw are not aware! Again, you absolutely *know* you are needed on *YOUTUBE*!

Fri Jun 27, 09:39:00 PM EDT

Anonymous said...

I am so glad we can post comments now! I so agree with you admonishing BW not to engage in wishful thinking. After my failed marriage to a BM about 5 years ago, I decided to open up my options to non-BM. I am under no illusion that a BM is going to wake up and start appreciating BW and am not waiting around for my 'Black Prince Charming' to rescue me. I am the only BW in my group of friends to have dated non-bm. I find that most BW are afraid, intimidated, and have such low self-esteem as to think they should only settle for dating DBR Black Men. Not taking the road that is expected of me (dating/marrying a BM) can be a lonely path indeed.

Fri Jun 27, 10:38:00 PM EDT

Maris said...

I saw a website today about another bw in Korea. I wish they had translated what she was saying. I saw a show where a Korean businessman fell in love with an African sister (Congolese) and married her. They have 2 children—a boy and a girl. We get love everywhere and we're not even aware of it! After all, Iman, Naomi Campbell, Gabrielle Union and Liyah Kebedeh are adored worldwide and are also sex symbols.

Sat Jun 28, 08:09:00 AM EDT

Nel said...

Evia, welcome back. You hit the nail on the head with this

one. Also, like you said: isn't it ironic that Barack Obama—who I too presume was not raised in a household in which black womens' looks were discounted—found love and happiness and a wonderful spouse in the very brown-skinned and uber cultured and educated Michelle Obama. Speaks volumes.

Sat Jun 28, 11:26:00 AM EDT

Victor said...

One of the regulars at my website emailed this link to your site to me. I actually somewhat touched on this topic on Tuesday.

Although I can't concur with much of what you say, I do agree with your overall premise. I've exclusively dated black women my entire life, yet I have no problem with sistas exploring and being open to their options. In fact, I encourage it. Our time on this planet is too transient to let something like race harness you when attempting to find a compatible romantic partner.

Sat Jun 28, 11:28:00 AM EDT

Anonymous said...

Evia, just wanted to say I really enjoy reading your blogs, and this is coming from a woman who has never dated outside her race. I agree with much of what you say about opening our options, but most of what I like about your blog doesn't even relate to dating. Your *living well* message, and 'bw as mules' messages are ones that every black woman needs to hear.

Sat Jun 28, 07:53:00 PM EDT

Phenombw said...

Hey Evia, I love all of your posts and I keep up with them. Even when you were on vacation, I was checking frequently. ☺

This is an excellent post. I love Michelle Obama, and I must admit I voted for him just to see Michelle as First Lady. I need to note though I think the supposed jealousy that darker black women like myself have for lighter skinned women is not legitimate, IMO.

My ex-best friend was light-skinned and we had no problems. I think people would be surprised to know how often it is actually the other way around. I have experienced a lot of jealousy and reminding that as darker skinned women, I'm not first-pick—from light-skinned women. Especially, when you are a gorgeous dark skinned women, it seems lighter-skinned women will try to make this known one way or another. Lol! That what's called "playing on one's self esteem." Doesn't work with me though. I just wanted to put that out there, because I've heard of this so-called jealousy that darker women have for lighter so many times and I personally totally disagree with it, because we beautiful darker skinned women see a different truth of this matter.

Sat Jun 28, 08:31:00 PM EDT

Lena said...

Imagine my surprise when I saw that one could comment. I pretty much agree with all you said in this post. Some months ago, I clicked to a black site through a link (the one where some silly black dude was saying that "Barack should control his 'Ho'). Not a single black man on this site called him out, except one black male poster at the end (there were several hundred posts).

What did amuse me, however, was what one poster said. On

the positives of an Obama presidency, he didn't see that it would encourage black children (well, boys) to aim higher, or that it would improve the image of black Americans around the world etc. No. The only benefit he could mention, and he was quite enthusiastic about it, was that *'Obama being in the White House will make white girls want to date us.'*

I actually shook my head and laughed. What made it even sadder was that the other numerous black men on this site seemed to agree. This was on a black site, where I'm sure most of these men would be mostly dating black women. Yet, that was what they saw as most beneficial of an Obama presidency.

I wonder why they didn't think Michelle being in the White House would make more *brothas* want to date black women, After all, would they not want to emulate the president?

And on the issue of black women thinking that bm will 'come home,' they know this is not going to happen. However, it gives these bw some sort of deluded hope, something to cling to. It's sad, really. I'm not too bothered by the obviously and openly damaged bm who do despicable things to sisters. What really gets me are the so-called "good" ones who sit by and say nothing, or somehow try to make the bm the victim. How such men are referred to as "good" completely baffles me. As far as I'm concerned, they are just as bad!

Sat Jun 28, 11:48:00 PM EDT

Evia said...

There are so many valuable and insightful points in some of the comments here that I'd like to address, but time limits me, so I can only address a few of them.

I need to note though I think the supposed jealousy that darker black women like myself have for lighter skinned women is not legitimate, IMO.

My ex-best friend was light-skinned and we had no problems. I think people would be surprised to know how often it is actually the other way around. I have experienced a lot of jealousy and reminding that as darker skinned women, I'm not first-pick—from light-skinned women.

Glad to hear that you don't hate on lighter women, but I think you mentioned at another point in your comment that you are a "beautiful" dark skinned woman. I'm assuming you've probably been told this many times by others? Gabrielle Union is considered a "beautiful" dark-skinned woman also. I hear this constantly said. Well, you and she are at the upper or extreme end of the "looks" scale. The bulk of people of any group are in the middle of the "looks" scale and have *average* looks.

White women who are in the middle are perfectly fine and acceptable among their men, and most average looking ww are considered attractive by typical African-American men due to internalized racism. However, African-American women who are in the middle (Serena Williams types) are mostly marked "down" by many bm and the ones considered closer to the other end (those considered unattractive) go through pure social hell at the hands of the "brothas" these days.

Many bm mark *up* an average looking ww since she has white skin and straight hair that can *blow in the wind*. But let's drill deeper here and examine this dark-skinned women vs light-skinned women friction. Many bw with average looks who look something like Serena Williams (facially) barely get noticed/asked out by many bm in this country.

A lot of bw who look like more like Mariah, Beyonce, and such get noticed/asked out/pursued, and have *many* more opportunities with all stripes of black men. Even Michelle would be overlooked by gobs of bm if she were not *'First Lady, Michelle Obama'* because—without being dolled-up, she falls in the average-looking range.

I'm not saying that light-bright black women don't have problems with bm. I'm saying they have many more opportunities with all types of bm and this is where much of the envy from *some* darker women is coming from. For ex, many AA men don't demand as much from a light-skinned bw because she brings *light skin* to his table. There are examples of that in my own family. No one wants to have fewer opportunities, especially for a superficial reason like skin shade or hair texture and length, etc. Isn't that why black men bitterly criticize racism which is a severe form of skin shade discrimination?

Many times, a lighter-brighter woman can have very average looks or less-than, dumpy looks and have clear character flaws, but she gets marked "up" by bm simply because she's lighter. In some cases, if she has the longish, straighter type of hair, then OMG, many AA men consider her a prize.

I'm considered a little bit light by some bm in the wintertime, so I've personally experienced how bm really love the lightness in a woman's skin because a man will let slip at some point why he's attracted to a woman and why she appeals to him. Lots of men may try to hide this, but a woman can glean this at some point. I've experienced this focus on my skin shade with several bm that I dated earlier in my life. They really *liked* my light butterscotch skin shade in the winter. Those same men wouldn't have been nearly as attracted to me, or not at all, if my skin was several shades darker, like it is in the summer. LOL!

Of course, some lighter women may be jealous of some darker women, especially if the darker woman looks like Gabrielle. But how many lighter women would be jealous of a Whoopi Goldberg type of bw. I mention Whoopi because so many bm have called her *ugly* and ridiculed her looks.

When the day comes that *most* African-American women realize that many AA men are looking at them and evaluating their beauty and worth through permanently "damaged" eyes, and reject the opinions of the men, that will spell *f-r-e-e-d-o-m* for so many sistas. Many bw think they're *less-than* because many bm think they're less-than.

Social scientists have proven that practically all people form their opinion of themselves—about their looks and their value— by viewing themselves through the eyes of others in their environment. You would *not* think that you're beautiful if you'd heard all of your life that you're *ugly*—especially from males.

If only lots more bw could simply ignore or discount the opinions of damaged and intolerant bm about them! Once they can do that, then they will be able to move towards quality men in the global village who *can* see their beauty and worth clearly.

Sun Jun 29, 10:50:00 AM EDT

Evia said...

> *I'm not too bothered by the obviously and openly damaged bm who do despicable things to*

sisters. What really gets me are the so-called "good" ones who sit by and say nothing, or somehow try to make the bm the victim. How such men are referred to as "good" completely baffles me. As far as I'm concerned, they are just as bad!

Thank you! This is a brilliant observation and I'm so happy you've pointed it out. This just goes to show how low some AAs have sunk in their *standards*—to label a man "good" simply because he doesn't actively attack bw. How in the world is a bm *passivity* considered *good* when black women and children are under constant attack, physically and psychologically?

If the "good" bm are indeed the majority of bm as so many bw and bm rush to remind me, then why is it that this majority of "good" bm are doing next to nothing to defend and protect us? What is their value to women and children? What purpose do they serve if they don't protect women and children? This is such illogical thinking. Are bm only good for sex?

I rarely even hear of blogs, websites, or print media where the "good" bm are vigorously fighting bw's verbal assailants. I'm not even talking about protecting bw from physical attacks—but the verbal ones. I get so sick and tired of African-Americans saying about bm, *"Well, at least he ain't in jail or on drugs or hittin' somebody in the head!"*

Well, damn! He's not *supposed* to be doing any of those things! Lots of AAs think that's a "normal," sensible comment, but widespread comments such as those clearly illustrate a kind of degeneration that can only have *one* end.

This is why I'm not swayed by the opinions of black folks who want me to shut up. It's clear to me that a lot of AAs (and some among other blacks too) have lost their minds. I am never going to be swayed in my perspectives by the opinions of these *crazies*.

When I first pointed out about a year and a half ago, that there was a growing number of damaged beyond repair black men out there among blacks who regarded the rest of us as sitting prey and that bw had better be on guard and also look elsewhere for loving and lovable men, many bw and bm verbally toasted me in online forums. The totally ironic thing is that *now*, some of those *same* bw (who were my worst critics) are now talking about arming themselves with *guns* against these DBRbm predators!

Some of my critics were actually saying, "How dare you call *our* men DBRs?" I guess they thought I was hurting the feelings of these predators? I dunno.

In actuality, those predators have more respect for me than they do for many of the bw who coddle them. The DBRs may hate me, but they respect me. They don't respect many, many of those coddling bw or bm who constantly make excuses for them.

Sun Jun 29, 11:30:00 AM EDT

Spring said...

> *Some of my critics were actually saying, "How dare you call our men DBRs?" I guess they thought I was hurting the feelings of these predators? I dunno.*

There is no "our men," and it is time most of us realized this fact. They always use the ever tiresome argument about how their fathers, brothers, uncles, cousins, blah, blah, blah, are black men too and how they love them. I'm really happy for them and how much they love the bm in their family but no one was referring to *them*. We were referring to the bm we have had negative personal experiences with—the general group of black men who behave in that way.

So, I don't know what the bm in their family have to do with our experiences with bm or the general group of bm who behave in a seriously subpar way. There are a *lot* of them, not just a small percentage. Maybe they recognized one of their bm relatives in some of our stories when we were sharing them. I, too, dunno.

Sun Jun 29, 02:17:00 PM EDT

Evia said...

> *They always use the ever tiresome argument about how their fathers, brothers, uncles, cousins, blah, blah, blah are black men too and how they love them.*

There are bm in my family who I love, but I don't confuse my loved ones with DBRbm out there who are doing this dirt. I, too, have bm in my family who are DBRs. I can clearly see a difference between their behavior and the ones who aren't. Why can't these other bw see the difference?

I was never talking about the bm in their families—unless they were predators, as you mentioned. And if I have predators in my family, I *want* somebody to point them out because a predator does not discriminate who they prey on. It could be me or anybody else.

The fact is that *many* young females are preyed on sexually, everyday, by male relatives and other familiar men who are pedophiles.

I'm really happy for them and how much they love the bm in their family but no one was referring to them. We were referring to the bm we have had negative personal experiences with—the general group of black men who behave in that way.

Yes, many bw have been preyed on by these DBRs, but in some cases, some of us may not have had the negative experience personally. That doesn't mean we don't know about what's going on or that we can't empathize with other women who are having the experience. If all women stop having empathy for other women, then bw will really be in the soup! Who is protecting bw?

It has been recognized that women in every culture and society from time immemorial need to be protected from predatory males. There are predatory males in *every* group— every day, all day long, but AA women overwhelmingly mingle with AA men. That's why I don't talk about DBR Chinese men, for ex., or other DBR men in this context. The first line of protection has *always* been the males from that woman's group. In the case of most AA girls and women, that first line of protection does *not* exist, and the predators know that. So, you can figure out the rest.

So, I don't know what the bm in their family have to do with our experiences with bm or the general group of bm who behave in a seriously subpar way.

That was merely a kneejerk reaction from some of those bw. Remember that many bw have been conditioned to protect and defend bm, and to *self-sacrifice* themselves, if necessary. In other cases, they were simply coddling bm. A lot of this is just automatic. When you talk with some bw about irresponsible bm, just notice how quickly the defense of bm starts. I've tested this. In defending the DBRs, bw are sista soldiers trying to *save the black community.*

Some of them try to bargain with bm by saying, *"Look, y'all, we love y'all to pieces, so y'all be good."*

That means nothing to the DBRs and predators, except it gives them the green light. You can't bargain with DBR people.

> *Maybe they recognized one of their bm relatives in some of our stories when we were sharing them.*

Magical thinking manifests itself in all kinds of ways, but it changes nothing and only fuels more behavior that is predatory.

Sun Jun 29, 03:55:00 PM EDT 🗑

Anonymous said...

AMEN, AMEN, and AMEN. I don't think I have ever read a better commentary or analysis on what the "typical" AA woman faces when it comes to dating and marrying a bm. I think the latest statistics on AA marriage is that only 28% of AA women are married! That is really sad to me. As a 32-year-old, AA woman, never married, no kids, homeowner, this really hits home.

I just ended a three-year relationship with a bm who was considered "successful" by society's standards. I am now in a relationship with a biracial white/Hispanic guy, and I am a lot happier. I find it interesting that the bm I was with earned less than half of what my current beau earns, yet since it was in the six figures, he considered himself a prime *catch.*

In his eyes, I was lucky to be with him. This same bm has three kids, a crazy ex-wife who attacked me, and horrible credit. ☺ My current boyfriend makes twice as much and calls himself an ordinary guy.

I'm a typical, right smack in the middle of the color spectrum AA female, whose skin color varies w/the seasons, like a lot of bw. Throughout my life, my hair length has also varied, due to medication, stress, etc. I have always had men of other races approach me no matter what phase of life I'm in. BM, on the other hand, tend to approach me too, Evia, more in the winter (lighter skin) and/or when my hair is permed and not in braids. Not other guys!

It's ironic that when guys of other races prefer black women, they tend to have a much wider range in their preferences, whereas bm tend to only want AA women on the lighter/whiter spectrum, if they want us at all!

I'm enjoying my new relationship to the fullest, and I encourage other AA women to date outside the race. Staying faithful to bm on the slim hope they will come "back" to us on their hands and knees is futile.

Evia, you are on point when it comes to *some* bm being *damaged beyond repair*. First, we must acknowledge this to ourselves. Then we must teach our daughters to recognize these predators. Then we must show our daughters the wide range of possible mates in the global village!

On the other side of the coin, we need to acknowledge the racial hatred and legacy still left in this country when those of other races deal with us. There is still a significant proportion of men of other races who will have sex with us, but not bring us home to mama! Personally, I flat out ask men of other races about their dating past. I want to know if they've dated bw before, how long have they been dating bw, do they date other/their own race, why do they want to date bw, etc, etc. I want to make sure this is not a superficial *rite of passage* or convenient *friends-with-benefits* relationship. Bw, if you get with a guy from another race, do the same thing!

Sun Jun 29, 04:30:00 PM EDT 🗑

Spring said...

> *That was merely a kneejerk reaction from some of those bw. Remember that many bw have been conditioned to protect and defend bm, and to self-sacrifice themselves if necessary. In other cases, they were simply coddling bm. A lot of this is just automatic.*

I was a lurker on a lot of these interracial relationship sites for a long time before I started posting and it was really disappointing reading the responses from bw protecting bm.

Meanwhile, none of them were involved with bm! It just didn't make sense, but like you said, a lot of bw were indoctrinated at an early age to protect and defend bm. So, I can understand why there was a kneejerk action to this. It must have felt like the third wall had been torn down. But, someone had to "pull the trigger" because the situation between bm and bw had really gotten out of hand.

However, I have noticed that they are trying to see things from a different perspective now (with very little magical thinking). I hope we can all move forward from here and just concentrate on the betterment of bw and bw only.

Sun Jun 29, 06:29:00 PM EDT 🗑

Alexis said...

I think I enjoy reading the comments section more than the main blog posts. I was on the BWWDI (Black Women Who Date Interracially) site, and a lady from LA was asking about encouraging her readers to date interracially. She seemed very concerned about her female readers. I suggested that she have a mixer where her readers can meet non-black men especially in LA. A lot of interracial dating is going on there.

My concern was a reply from one of our regulars who said that she should not push black women into dating interracially. Another one said she should because they need to know there are alternatives.

I wonder if you get email from women who are on the fence about interracial dating? What do you tell them?

Sun Jun 29, 10:53:00 PM EDT 🗑

Evia said...

> *I can honestly say that I have never felt a need to defend bm in anyway because I don't believe in looking out for those who aren't looking to help further my interest.*

This was the point of this post—to say to black woman once again that the evidence clearly shows that the masses of AA men *these days* are *not* looking out for bw's and black children's interests.

However, I don't know about the bw y'all encounter, but most of the ones I hear talking about these various issues still believe that the masses of bm are *actively* on our side. They continue to believe the 'talk' of the males when they talk about all the *supposed* love they have for black women or that talk where bm refer to bw as "our queens." Forget that! Talk is nothing! Where's the *action?*

Some of those women definitely believe that bw need to find more ways to show our allegiance to bm because they are *our* men. SMH By helping to send a black boy to college, for ex., the women believe that their contributions are creating black husbands and fathers for black women. The fact is that this was true in the past, maybe 40 years ago and beyond, but not now. This is increasingly *not* true these days, and we're living *now.*

A black male college graduate *these days* who gets good employment is more than likely to date, cohabit with, and/or marry a nonblack woman. Look at the stats and notice how many bm college graduates and other 'rising' bm are marrying or committing themselves and their resources to *non-black* women. Researchers and statisticians track all of this, so it's all published. Or, these men are not marrying *anyone.*

Tell me which other group of women would continue to pump their resources into the men of their group when the men more than likely will not marry women from that community or share the resources with women from their group? Yet, the masses of AA women are still following the old *"build up a bm"* program. SMH! We need different ways for different days.

Black political "leaders" (men and women) and local community *thought leaders* are still beating the *help a black man* drum everywhere I turn, expressing all of this concern about what is happening to black males. So, lots of bw believe, without question, that if black males rise, they will put bw up there on the pedestal with them. That's an assumption.

This is why I point out that as much as some bm (bw too) bash Obama and claim that he's not "really" a bm, he has put a *black* queen on the highest pedestal of all. He didn't just talk about how he "loves the sistas" as so many bm do, who then run out and find the most *un-sista* looking woman they can find.

It doesn't matter to me *why* Obama chose Michelle because smart people don't judge others by their thoughts or feelings, they judge them by their *actions.* So Obama's selection of Michelle for his wife and the mother of his children was a very significant *action* because she's a symbol. Symbolism is very important in propaganda (poisonous information) wars and there is much poison in the media that crushes the spirits of black females at this point. I'm not saying that people sit in rooms and plot how to deliberately attack bw. It doesn't matter whether it's deliberate or collateral damage; it is what it is. Bw lack immunity or defensive shields against the poison, so it invades the psyches of many black girls and bw.

I know Obama didn't choose Michelle to help bw out—☺— but this action did help tremendously to strengthen the spirits, the morale of countless black females. If your spirit is strong, you can do the rest on your own. If your spirit is weak, you can be easily mowed down.

I don't know what his policies will be, but I know that he knows that his policies will have a direct effect on his wife and the destines of his daughters as black females in a sexist country that has many racial structures in place, so I do believe that he will do his best to look out for their welfare. That, in itself, is guaranteed to help the rest of us black females in small and large ways.

Likewise, when a bw marries a wm, that bw has influence on his decisions, directly and indirectly, and if he's a well-positioned wm, her marriage to him will often indirectly and directly help other black women because we're all connected.

Let's look at this: If wm do indeed have *all or the major portion* of the power and influence, as so many black folks keep saying, then instead of looking at a bw who marries a wm as having "escaped," the black "community" should applaud that bw because she's now in a much better position to access the power. Her access to power will indirectly and directly benefit other blacks—even if she doesn't care about black folks. For sure, when women in other ethnic and racial communities (for ex. Asian women) marry white men, their communities regard those marriages exactly like that! They regard the marriages as elevating the women—and indirectly their ethnic or racial community.

Mon Jun 30, 07:38:00 AM EDT 🗑

Evia said...

> *I think I enjoy reading the comments section more than the main blog posts.*

This is exactly why I opened up the comments section again so that commenters can share their valuable insight here.

> *I was on the Black Women Who Date Interracially site, and a lady from LA was asking about encouraging her readers to date interracially.*

I encourage bw to broaden their options only "if" they're not satisfied with their present options. This is common sense.

> *She seemed very concerned about her female readers. I suggested that she have a mixer where her readers can meet non-black men especially in LA. A lot of interracial dating is going on there.*
>
> *My concern was a reply from one of our regulars who said that she should not push black women into dating interracially.*

"Push?" Hmmm. If you mean *pressure*, I certainly agree that bw should *not* be *pressured*. I don't think any woman should be pressured to date any man if she doesn't want to do it.

> *Another one said she should because they need to know there are alternatives.*

I believe that bw definitely need to know about as many of their dating and marriage options/alternatives as possible, or as many as we can find out about and present to them. Thus, my blog.

> *I wonder if you get email from women who are on the fence about interracial dating? What do you tell them?*

Actually, I don't get e-mail from bw who are "on" the fence. 99.9% of the mail I get is from bw who already know they want to get *over* the fence or they're thanking me for already helping them get over the fence. So, they've already decided.

There are many factors that motivate me to continue to blog, but that one is a biggie—the large volume of mail I get from women who write that my message *frees their mind*, supports, uplifts them, and confirms their decision. I tell ya, it's such a beautiful feeling to know that my words can actually help to *free* somebody's mind!

I do encounter many bw in my offline life who express frustrations about loneliness or the poor quality of men they meet. I just present all the options and benefits to them of broadening their mating pool. I don't try to *push* them to take advantage of these options. I've noticed that many bw—at all socioeconomic levels— have very limited information about their options and opportunities across the board and usually lack the support to pursue unfamiliar options.

I love it when others give me info about more options and opportunities, so I try to do the same thing.

If you keep presenting relationship options and benefits to women who have fairly good emotional health and normal intelligence, and if they know they will get *support*, many of them will eventually make the best choice for themselves. After we have offered them information and *support*, if they choose to remain *on the fence* or are not interested in movement, we have to accept that as their decision. We each have been given free will.

Support is a biggie. We don't talk nearly enough about bw "supporting" each other because the main focus has been—up until now—on bw supporting bm.

Excuse me for going off on this tangent, but just think: if many bw reading this had enough support from other bw today, they could set up wildly successful businesses. They could win high political offices, set up boarding schools around the country to rescue some of the black girls who live in these hell-hole neighborhoods and teach them to love themselves and empower them (like Oprah's doing in South Africa). Others could effectively start up or sponsor media that could bring to a trickle the assaults on bw, and on and on. We could do these things *today,* if we supported each other enough and *knew* that support was there. Many bw have the know-how to do all these things and more, but without the support from each other, we flounder.

Mon Jun 30, 08:48:00 AM EDT 🗑

Yvette said...

Excellent, excellent, excellent !

Mon Jun 30, 10:01:00 AM EDT 🗑

Evia said...

Skimming through the comments, I saw this from an Anon.

> *On the other side of the coin, we need to acknowledge the racial hatred and legacy still left in this country when those of other races deal with us.*

I *never* ignore that this country has lots of entrenched racism, but I prefer to focus on the glass as half-full.

Not aimed at you, but I think that too many blacks spend too much time and tons of energy focusing on why we "can't do" this or that instead of talking, writing, researching, detailing, teaching, encouraging, and in other words focusing on *how-to* to be more effective at doing what we need to do in order to 'Live Well.'

I think this is an element of my message that some folks clearly don't understand. They don't understand why I don't talk more about racism and they want me to slice and dice racist white men and women on the regular. But I think there are enough black folks out there already who rip racism. That's the focus of their blogs, books, speeches, etc. After decades of doing that and thousands of books, conferences, speeches, things have gotten worse for typical African Americans, IMO.

So, there's a lot of heat and *no light* out there for millions of black people! I could easily bash *'de evil wm and ww,'* but at the end of the day, nothing will have changed. So I decided to do something much more practical—help to emotionally uplift bw and present new options to help heterosexual bw to deal with a particular deficit area in their lives: a loving and lovable quality man.

I was raised to succeed both *despite* and *because* of racism. So the fact that gazillions of whites may not like me or don't appreciate me or think I'm inferior and might do their utmost to keep me down doesn't make me pause. I feel the same way about black men who don't appreciate me. I don't care! People like that can never get inside me. I am emotionally immune to them and I wish other bw could develop that immunity.

IMO, racist whites and bm haters of black women suffer from a peculiar form of mental illness because the hate is only triggered when we don't bow down, defer to them, and/or serve their needs. Think about it. If we bowed down, deferred to them, and served them, racist whites would approve of blacks and hateful bm would love black women once again. ☺

My mission is to figure out a way to get what I want out of life or *live well* no matter who doesn't like me and I always keep in mind that there are also many people out there who *do* like and appreciate me. That's the glass half-full. So these are the folks I focus on.

> *There are still a significant proportion of men of other races that will have sex with us, but*

not bring us home to mama!

The way I look at this and handled this was I "knew" that having sex with a man was not going to make him care about me. I *knew* that—whether he was black, nonblack, or whatever. That part really needs to sink into a woman's head and she'll then realize that sex has nothing to do with him taking her home to meet his mama. If a grown woman wants to have sex with a man, she should just protect herself, have it, and know that in *most* instances, it's just a pleasurable "release" for a man, especially if she's barely into a relationship with him. *Sex, alone, does not cause a man to want to commit to a woman.*

I advocate that a woman should always steer the relationship since she has more to lose. First should come the "relationship-building" which takes *time,* where she gives the man ample opportunities to know her mind and heart, and bond with her in a non-sexual way. She should behave in a lighthearted, flirtatious, engaging way, but not cling. She should show her affectionate nature to a man—if she likes him—and there can even be some light intimacy during this phase (initial 5 or 6 dates). This gives him a preview of the physical relationship later on. Some of you might think this is old-fashioned, but this is an effective mode of behavior for steering a relationship towards a long-term commitment.

Jumping between the sheets with a man who is not marriage-minded, marriage-ready, or one who has not bonded with a woman emotionally and mentally, rarely works.

The more I read about this overriding *concern* or fear from bw that wm *only* wants sex, the more I'm beginning to believe that bw don't seem to be able to control their *own* libidos. LOL!

It doesn't matter what *any* man wants physically from a woman, a woman doesn't have to give it to him. She should give him a chance to get to know her first and she, him. If he doesn't want to stick around for that, then she hasn't lost anything even if he doesn't take her home to meet his mama.

Mon Jun 30, 10:51:00 AM EDT 🗑

Yvette said...

Just check out articles about "hottest sports couples." Very few top black athletes are associated with black women. Those who do have bw as girlfriends and wives have selected light, bright, and damn near white women.

Bw, it's a new day. Bw ought to be taking advantage of *all* of *their* options, whenever they can, just like bm are doing. Notice that an *average* looking white woman is more likely to marry a wealthy, successful black man than a "cream of the crop" black woman.

Mon Jun 30, 11:03:00 AM EDT 🗑

Yvette said...

> *How odd while we, as blacks, are basking in the 'I'm proud of a black man' moment, we are forgetting one crucial element. And the main reason I suspect white people are voting for him is despite his color Obama was raised in a white household. The crucial element is that his experience isn't uniquely a traditional Black experience. . . .*

But one thing that you have to realize is that regardless of the fact that he is biracial and Harvard educated, the man is *afrocentric*. He married a bw. He could have had his 'pick of the litter.' He not only picked a bw; he thinks that she is fabulous. A dark skinned bw. A regular-looking bw. I am sure that a lot of black men look at him and wonder why he does not have a white/light woman. Trust me they do.

In addition, regardless of how crazy the Reverend Wright may be, he has a very *afrocentric* church. Obama was entrenched with regular black folks, like us. I love and have so much respect for him.

Mon Jun 30, 11:12:00 AM EDT 🗑

Spring said...

> It doesn't matter what ANY man wants, a woman doesn't have to give it to him. She should give him a chance to get to know her first and she, him. If he doesn't want to stick around for that, then she hasn't lost anything even if he doesn't take her home to meet his mama.

Evia, I totally cosign. This is great advice. I am in my early thirties and the dating world has really changed, in the last ten years. It seems that woman have very little virtue or self-respect. I get it—you're sexually liberated when it comes to sex. I am a bit old-fashioned when it comes to sex and dating. I will not give "it" up until I am in a serious relationship and when I tell most men this, they look at me as if I am some kind of alien from an uncharted planet.

I believe women teach men how to treat us in some respects. If most women in today's society are willing to have sex with a man they hardly know, it ruins it for women like me who want to be taken seriously, first. I have to say that I am getting really sick of the *Sex and the City* wanna-be behavior of today's women.

Mon Jun 30, 11:53:00 AM EDT 🗑

Yvette said...

> *I find it interesting that the bm I was with earned less than half of what my current beau earns, yet since it was in the six figures, he considered himself a prime catch. In his eyes, I was lucky to be with him.*

I dated for about a year a very successful, divorced, African physician who was very well-off financially. He was not attractive at all. The average black woman would not look at him if he were out. But you know what? He *knew* his value as a successful black physician, despite his looks. I have seen some of the black women he has dated and they are beautiful and successful. He knew that he did not have to do much for these women and that another would just come along. He also has two sons who are being raised (by his successful ex wife) in an affluent community. He knows that his sons will most likely marry and date white women and he really does not care.

Also, I went out with a gorgeous, successful, black man last week. I meet good-looking, successful black men all the time. The thing is that attractive, educated, black woman are a dime a dozen to these successful black men—ugly or fine. They have lots and lots of women to choose from. Therefore, I have taken myself out of the game. So I don't even let it get further than a few dates because I know how things will turn out and *no sex*! I only go out with these guys while I am looking for a (preferably non-black guy) who really will care about *me and treat me well*!

Mon Jun 30, 12:02:00 PM EDT 🗑

Yvette said...

> *The fact is that this is not exactly true. A black male college graduate these days that gets good employment is more than likely to date, cohabit with, and/or marry a nonblack woman. Look at the stats and notice how many bm college graduates and other 'rising' bm are with nonblack women. These men are using their resources to help provide comfortable lives for women in other groups to a large extent.*

I have a good friend who graduated from Morehouse College, and he said a quite a few really *good catches* (his classmates) are marrying white girls.

Mon Jun 30, 12:11:00 PM EDT 🗑

Evia said...

> *. . . when it comes to sex and dating. I will not give "it" up until I am in a serious relationship and when I tell most men this, they look at me as if I am some kind of alien from an uncharted planet.*

I call it being "sensible," not *old-fashioned*. If a woman and man both agree that they want a long-term relationship (LTR), there'll be plenty of time for sex later on.

However, if the woman just wants quickie sex too, then that's different. I have a male cousin who says that he meets women who will try to get him into bed on the first date. LOL! For ex., he said he'll be talking to them, trying to get to know them and they'll be rubbing up against him or making *suggestive* comments. I think some women think this is what they have to do to pull a man. They are way off target!

Once again, let me point out that the purpose of dating for a woman is to evaluate whether the man is suitable and compatible for a long-term committed relationship (marriage), if she's marriage-ready. She shouldn't just go out with a man because it's the weekend and she's bored. Btw, the key purpose of dating for the bulk of men (especially at younger ages) is to get sex. Women and men have very different primary goals for dating, and women are seemingly unaware of this.

Most mature-minded men (of any age) with good intentions towards a woman will understand and appreciate that a woman is not quickly sexual because if she does it with him quickly, she probably does it quickly with every man.

I don't have any problem suggesting a degree of sexual intimacy during the early point in a relationship though. There can be lots of affection and intimate "touching" if the couple talk about it first, *both* agree on the limits, and both take responsibility for maintaining the limits. It is important to agree on this in advance.

As usual, it's not *what* you do; it's *how* you do it.

Mon Jun 30, 12:26:00 PM EDT 🗑

Sonya said...

> *The more I read about this overriding "concern" or fear from bw that wm only wants sex, the more I'm beginning to believe that bw don't seem to be able to control their own libidos. LOL!*

I'm just going to comment on this one little bit of info I glimpsed. This is a big concern of mine. I understand that sex doesn't equal love, relationship, or anything like that with men. That's fine (though I don't like it one little bit). My problem is that I have needs and urges too. Despite what people say about bw, I am not "out there." The need builds up, especially if you are lacking in the relationship area and end up in a *dry spell.*

This can cloud your judgment when looking for a partner. Like I said before, I have needs too. But as a woman, sex does cause me to develop feelings. That's just how it is. So, what's a girl to do? This is very frustrating.

Mon Jun 30, 12:33:00 PM EDT 🗑

Evia said...

I want y'all to remember that I have a very marriage-oriented philosophy insofar as bw of a marriageable age are concerned, so if you're not a marriage-oriented woman or you're not at that stage of your life, then a lot of my perspectives may not apply.

Okay, let me get over to the gym. Darren does his workout early in the morning, but I get caught up with other things like yakking here and other stuff, and the day just slides by. ☺

Mon Jun 30, 12:35:00 PM EDT 🗑

Evia said...

My problem is that I have needs and urges too.

Sonya, if you're going to have sex to relieve your *needs and urges*, just protect your heart and your body. Also, there is such a thing as *self-pleasuring.* It's not optimal, but it's preferable to putting yourself in a position where you can be used or abused by a man, if you're the type of woman who can't control her emotions.

But I can't answer this for you or any other woman. I can only make suggestions which I strongly believe will serve a woman well. You don't *have to* get emotional about the man. Stop telling yourself that. I think that sometimes women hear that 'women are supposed to' be a certain way and just think that they're helpless. Not true. Many men have certain women in their lives just for sex, though most men won't tell the woman that's all she is to them. Men usually decide very early in the interaction that that's all that the woman can be to them because she's not suitable for them in other ways, and so it is. Take a page from that book and work hard on shaping yourself in that way, that is, if you have to succumb to your urges.

Mon Jun 30, 03:28:00 PM EDT 🗑

Phenombw said...

> *IMO, racist whites and bm haters of black women suffer from a peculiar form of mental illness because the hate is only triggered when we don't bow down, defer to them, and/or serve their needs. Think about it. If we bowed down, deferred to them, and served them, racist whites would approve of blacks and hateful bm would love black women once again. LOL!*

This is so true, Evia.

To Sonya: I understand being young, it can be hard to control your urges. I'm in my mid 20's and I've been abstaining from having sex for many years now. The reward in doing this is you get to know yourself better. It's harder for just any man to come into your life. Most of the men I've dated I've kept an open minded with, but if I know they cannot make me happy emotionally I move on.

You see, when you stop wanting a man to complete you sexually (by being abstinent) you start looking for the more important lifelong connections with a man. Believe me, it will be very easy to not have sex—because once you truly know and understand self, you become choosier.

Being a single mom and going to school, committing to abstinence has assured me only the one child I have and most importantly, I feel so empowered. This is something I have control over and have controlled. So when you feel the need to have sex, just read a book, go to the gym, or find a hobby. Eventually, it will become a habit to not dwell on. But, also know when you do find that special someone that built up sexual energy will knock his socks off. LOL! I'm anticipating that day.

Mon Jun 30, 07:37:00 PM EDT 🗑

Sele said...

Hey Sis, I've missed you, however I've lurked around some of your comments on another blog. ☺

Like Miss Pin said, I've been hearing the same thing from bw in regards to Obama's *powers* to change or encourage bm to do the "right thing". If Jesus, Moses, and MLK can't make a bm grow up, who the heck is Obama? LOL

Mon Jun 30, 11:36:00 PM EDT 🗑

Maris said...

> *There is still a significant proportion of men of other races that will have sex with us, but not bring us home to mama!*

I completely understand this fear but I see it like this: I don't know anything that some non-black men do that most black men didn't/don't do to us, which I find worse, personally. In general, what I often hear is: *"All that non-bm want to do is have sex with us." The* majority of bm only want sex from bw too. No marriage, no taking care of their kids. That's why they hate Barack and Bill Cosby for exposing these truths. Also, on the *Tyra* Banks show a few months ago, a bm was exposed for saying to one of *Tyra's* employees behind the scene that bm do use bw for sex. That happened in the "BW vs BM" edition of the *Tyra* Banks show.

Then I sometimes hear, *"Non-bm hate and disrespect us."* The only people who constantly call us b*tches and h*es are bm. I mean even offline, I have yet to be called the B-word and H-word by a non-bm. On the other hand, I've been called everything but a child of God by my own kind, ridiculed on TV by D.L. Hughley (in the Rutgers girls/*Don Imus* situation), and that man refused to apologize.

The men who constantly perpetrate the "bw are only good for sex" stereotype are bm. Just listen to today's music. There's no other race of men that diss their women on YouTube but bm. No other race of men would mobilize in NYC to diss their women *openly* and threaten to harm them but bm. A bm on *Youtube* made a video about it and urged bw to quit being *loyal* to bm.

The reality is that a man of any race can respect or disrespect you. Maybe it's also a matter of experience, but trust me, I've met so many respectful non-bm in my life. Many non-bm see our struggle and see us rising in spite of the obstacles; they take notice and therefore have major respect for us.

Tue Jul 01, 12:14:00 AM EDT 🗑

Sherry said...

I am so pleased to see Evia blogging and opening up the

comments. I'm just going to sit here for a moment and read and take in the comments and the positivity...and then I will keep doing what I'm doing...living well and thriving.

Welcome back, Evia

Tue Jul 01, 01:46:00 AM EDT 🗑

Joshua said...

Do white men want black women only for sex? Good question. Here's a better one: do they want white women for more than that either?

Face it—most of us are simply dogs, and black or white, the only thing that changes the fundamental nature of a man is his faith in and trust of God. So if you want more than "a good guy"—whatever that is—if you want a real man, find one that doesn't wait for *you* to tell *him* it's hands off till you're married. Find one that tells *you* that's how it's going to be before you even bring it up. Real men are leaders who don't wait for women to set a standard. Speaking as a white man and more importantly just as a man, at the end of the day, if you truly *love* a woman, you're going to be willing to wait.

Let me rephrase it like this, what man can claim he loves you if he's willing to compromise and damage your conscience and fill your heart with guilt and fear just because he has *needs?*

Answer: One who is lying to you. Refuse to accept anything less than the best. It's what you deserve and what God wants you to have.

Tue Jul 01, 03:39:00 AM EDT 🗑

Lena said...

> *However, I have noticed that they are trying to see things from a different perspective*

> *now (with very little magical thinking). I hope*
> *we can all move forward from here and just*
> *concentrate on the betterment of bw and bw*
> *only.*

I don't know if that comment was aimed at me, taking into account our back-and-forth on another blog. Please believe me, the opinions I have now are the same as I 've had for a long time. I just don't believe in double standards. I call black men out when they do it, hence, I also call out black women when they do it.

> *I am sure that a lot of brothers look at him*
> *and wonder why he does not have a white/light*
> *woman. Trust me they do.*

So true. On that site I was talking about, another black guy actually questioned why Obama hadn't married a white woman. In his head, Obama, being biracial, should have made it more likely for him to marry someone white or any other non-black woman. So this fellow wanted a black president but not a black first lady. I've even come across another foolish black male who said that he would have been more willing to vote for Obama if he had been married to a white woman. His logic was that he 'preferred the symbol that they would represent.' Sometimes, I just don't get some peoples' stupidity.

Tue Jul 01, 06:22:00 AM EDT 🗑

Lena said...

On the whole topic of DBR men, Ladies remember, if there exists DBR-bm, there also exists DBR-bw. Not every black woman is your friend. Just take a look at the bw who'd make comments like *'we won'* in reference to R. Kelly getting off for raping that 14-year-old girl. Who the 'we' is, I'm not sure. And how this can be called *winning*, I'm not sure.

Tue Jul 01, 06:25:00 AM EDT 🗑

Hopeful said...

> *Also, I believe this helped him in choosing Michelle as a mate. He just saw a good, educated, beautiful woman who wanted the same things in life he did. Like I said, his upbringing was vastly different than most bm. Not to take away from his accomplishments, but the black community shouldn't try to latch on to this like this will and can magically turn our communities around.*

I have to agree with that. One of the things I have noticed in this campaign was how many votes Barack Obama got from white men and young people. Hillary got a lot of support from mostly white women, also a lot of feminists. Obviously, a lot of men are looking at Michelle Obama. She will be on the world stage. An elderly ww said that if Michelle wasn't married to Barack, she would push for her daughter to marry Obama.

Look how those women screamed when Michelle was on *The View*. That black and white dress she wore sold out within minutes. She doesn't wear panty hose, so the cameras were on her legs. You wait until she gets into the White House. Black women are going to be in so much demand, the BC will be bawling. If you think that the BM and others in the BC are complaining about us now, you wait until November 2008, when Barack is elected.

Tue Jul 01, 07:11:00 AM EDT 🗑

Evia said...

> *The thing is that attractive, educated black woman are a dime a dozen to these successful black men—ugly or fine. They have lots and lots of women to choose from. . . . I removed myself from the game*

Very *shrewd* move because it is a "game" to many of the men, and women are treated like game pieces. Bw get treated worse because both my cousin and my bm friend say that bm know that most bw will try to stay on the game board for bm, no matter what.

> *So I don't even let it get further than a few dates because I know how things will turn out and no sex!*

Great! And when you walk away, you haven't left your self-respect behind.

At my women's group last night, one bw who had been "out there" for a while talked about how "soiled" she'd always feel the next morning, knowing she'd allowed a man who cared nothing about her, use her body.

> *I only go out with these guys while I am looking for a (preferably non-black) guy who really will care about me and treat me well!*

I've often talked about how I would casually date 2 or 3 men at the same time when I was dating, but there was *no sex* with any of them. I protected myself 'first and foremost.' Of course, I always would let them know indirectly that I was seeing other men because that's how I deal with men—in a *no-games* way—but I didn't tell any man much of my business and I knew he wasn't telling me everything either.

Several years ago, *ESSENCE* magazine also recommended this dating strategy and ran a lengthy article on it because too many bw have a tendency to become emotionally involved with men *way* too soon. Bw need to keep their emotions in check until a man has *proven* himself worthy.

Maybe, I just don't understand how bw (and other women too) can "love" all of these unworthy men! I can understand why the mamas of these guys would love their sons, but *puhlease!* I mean, what are these guys bringing to the table that would make a woman jeopardize her health, her heart, her future—like I see some women do. I really believe that one major reason some bw do this is because many bw do not believe they can find a *quality* man or that a quality man will want them. So they "settle." They fear that if they're selective, they'll end up with no one. They're right as long as they fish in a tiny pool.

This is why the biggest part of the solution is too present bw with a wide array of their relationship options. And bw, once you get this knowledge of the options, you can't just know this and keep it to yourself, you must talk about this to other unaware black women, and especially young black girls and teenage girls. Give them the information about choices, early!

If a bw believes (as many bw apparently do) that she doesn't have any choice but to date the loser/user man (even if he wears a 3-piece suit), then how can she be expected to make *better* choices? The *nothing-but-a-bm* indoctrination was presented to me early in my life, but it never took hold in me. I made good choices because I *knew* that I had lots of choices available to me, especially after I moved to a big city.

A lot of bw are still not telling other bw flat-out to *forget* about unworthy black men. When I was growing up and coming of age, my grandmother and mother didn't mince words. They taught me not to let any "no good" or unsuitable man get near me. They taught me what to look at to *vet* men. They didn't care about political correctness. So I was never confused and never had to deal with the man-problems that some bw go through.

Anyway, I discovered that dating 2 or more men at the same time was a type of unpressured fun and it's one of the best things a woman can do to prevent herself from spending too much time with any one man for the wrong reasons: loneliness, boredom, sex, etc. When you date two or more men simultaneously, you always have a man to go out with, and you don't spend too much time with or thinking about any of them, which can lead to having sex too early for some women or cause some women to think they're "in love."

Also, if one of the men starts messing up, you can cut him loose quickly and still have the other guys in your life. This strategy gives a woman the chance to meet other men since she's not pinned down with one man who's not suitable.

Usually what happens in this scenario is that one of the men will pull ahead of the others and *show* the woman (by his treatment of her) that he's the best choice. This is what I was doing when I met my first husband and my current one.

Also, this is standard operating procedure for many men, but men don't tell you this and many of them will criticize women for doing this and want to call her the h-word. ☺ They believe that a woman who dates a 2-3 men simultaneously is having sex with all of the guys because a man who dates several women at once is most definitely doing that or trying to do it.

Many men have women in their lives who are "placeholders," while they are looking for *Miss Right* and meanwhile the men are sexing the placeholders. They're usually leading her to believe that she's the only woman in their lives.

I'm not suggesting that women do this because men do it; I just see this as a common sense, win-win strategy for bw.

Tue Jul 01, 08:15:00 AM EDT 🗑

Evia said...

Hey Sele! Re:

> *If Jesus, Moses, and MLK can't make a bm grow up, who the heck is Obama? LOL*

So funny! Gurl! I'm not even expecting Obama to *walk on de water* for black folks. If he makes it to the White House, he'll be the President of *all* the people. So, I'm not expecting him to *'save alla our people.'* That's magical thinking.

I'd hope he'd make policy changes that would tear down those *invisible*, multi-layered racist *structures* that work against black progress. Blacks themselves, on an individual level, must do the rest. He can't come into peoples' homes and teach them how to raise their children. He can't teach black kids to value education and become intellectually fierce. He can't force a bm to be a responsible parent to his children. He can't stop young bm from killing each other, even if he puts a billion cops in the neighborhoods. He can force black folks to watch less TV or eat better and exercise more.

He can't change black folks' values and that's where most of the problems of black folks, these days, exists—in those counter-productive, counter-progressive values. Obama also can't force white people to "like" black people, as some bm apparently hope he can do, so that they can more easily get ww. He can't force blacks to develop networks, like other groups do, that help them to make progress either.

Obama can't stop bw from coddling, enabling, excusing, or catering unconditionally to bm which is what contributes to most of the disrespect and disdain heaped on bw by bm. The major reason bm don't respect bw is because bw don't demand reciprocity and are not willing to hang these men up by their testicles when they don't deliver.

White women and African women, for ex. are *generally* willing to hang a wm or African man out to dry, and fast, if he doesn't do his utmost to play his role as protector and provider. Many AA women continue to talk about how *'hard life is for a brotha'* or *'cutting a brotha some slack.'* They don't demand that a bm do his utmost. I mean, why can't a bm work 2-3 jobs if he needs to do it? Lots of bw work 2-3 jobs regularly, so why are bm any better than bw?

If we're going to be honest about it, there are currently already many opportunities that AAs don't take advantage of. AAs and other blacks need to examine themselves and admit that many of their own attitudes and behaviors limit them. Personally, I constantly evaluate my own attitudes and behaviors to determine whether I'm self-limiting or short-changing myself.

I've talked to some of my older relatives about the goals of the Civil Rights movement, integration, etc. because I wanted to find out what was really in the minds of black folks at that point.

The purpose of integration was to provide *access* to equal opportunities. The black folks of that era knew that was just the beginning! They knew that racist whites were still going to fight to limit them. They weren't looking for whites to accept, approve, validate, or love them.

But they were conned by "smooth talk," just like a lot of women get swayed by flowery words. They got played mostly by deceitful, self-serving other black people.

So, today we have many young blacks who pretend that they put the "t" in tough, yet will crumble and drop out of the university if white students there won't smile at them. ☹ Lawdy!

Obama is not a magician, but many blacks who engage in magical thinking will expect him to be.

Tue Jul 01, 09:24:00 AM EDT 🗑

Donnela said...

Yvette, I think white people always look for the black people who are exception to the rule. Trust me, I know. I spent most of my life being one. Even in grade school, high school, and work, I am told "You're not like other black people." I still take it as a insult. That's why I've always had an array of friends (female and male) who were racially diverse. Even my black ex-husband called me his 'white wife' because of my supposedly traditional, less drama-filled view on life.

My white fiancé called me the 'whitest' black girl he ever dated. And like Obama, I went to a black Christian church. I really don't see his afrocentric qualities. I just see an American man living out the traditional American values: faith in God, hard work, ambition, education, and family.

Obama for his part has lived what whites considered the traditional American life. He's not like the others because many whites feel blacks have too much drama in their life. They're more comfortable with him, than, say a Jesse Jackson.

Tue Jul 01, 09:32:00 AM EDT 🗑

Sele said...re:

> On the whole topic of DBR men, Ladies remember, if there exists DBR-bm, there also exists DBR-bw. Not every black woman is your friend. Just take a look at the bw who'd make comments like 'we won' in reference to R. Kelly getting off for raping that 14-year-old girl. Who the 'we' is, I'm not sure. And how this can be called winning, I'm not sure.

ITA. However, please believe me we have talked about DBRbw ad nauseam, specifically on Evia's blog. That's why, in the past, it's been quite puzzling why some folks accused Evia of man-bashing, etc. DBR-ism is a "group effort" of destruction. Why do you think most bw remain "chained" in the first place?

Evia did a wonderful piece a while back called the *Black Woman Card*. That post will more than echo exactly what you're saying!

Tue Jul 01, 09:36:00 AM EDT 🗑

Donnela said...

Also, the whole thing about educated bw being *a dime a dozen* is about to change. I see more and more bw, 25 and under succumbing to the stereotype of the gold-digging video vixen. So sad to say it, but after years of seeing the good black women without bm and seeing all the hood chicks with black men, a lot of our young black women are taking cues from pop culture.

They see how the sexy, brainless chick is more valuable in the black community than the smart black woman.

We should now spend our time changing the attitude of *nothing-but-a-bm* that is still so engrained in so many of our young girls' minds. I am doing this for my two daughters who see me date bm and wm. My 15-year-old is convinced she is going to marry either *Shia Labouf* or *Chris Brown*. She knows she has a choice.

Tue Jul 01, 09:50:00 AM EDT 🗑

Evia said...@ Lena re:

> *I don't know if that comment was aimed at me, taking into account our back-and-forth on another blog. . .*

Let's assume it wasn't. This is not a back-and-forth forum.

> *Please believe me, the opinions I have now are the same as I've had for a long time. I just don't believe in double standards. I call black men out when they do it; hence, I also call out black women when they do it.*

Also, I'm the one who made the initial comment here about how some bw—who didn't seem to be able to bear the thought of referring to many bm as "damaged" or DBRbm—are now talking about and/or co-signing arming themselves with *guns*—no less—to shoot these men, if these men attack them. It just seems to me to be a giant leap, so I commented on that.

But let's look at this DBRbm and DBRbw thing. First of all, this issue was discussed ad infinitum on Halima's blog and various commenters made the case compellingly that the DBR man is the much more destructive—of the two—to *other people*.

Males, in general, tend to "explode" or *act out* their damage (rape, maim, assault, molest, kill, etc.) whereas females, in general, tend to "implode" (overeating, excess sex, excess shopping, escapist sleeping, verbal abuse, sneaky behavior, passive aggressiveness, etc.). Of course, there's some overlapping in some cases. But I'm talking about general patterns here.

However, I'm not saying that *all* women who engage in some or all of these behaviors are DBRs.

So I know that there are DBRbw out there, but as I pointed out in my FAQs blog, I don't talk about or put emphasis on them because this is primarily a bw's relationship blog that discusses black women's relationships with *men* of various backgrounds. Heterosexual bw are not seeking a romantic relationship with any type of woman. So I certainly don't consider myself engaging in a double standard—just in case anyone is interested.

This blog is not geared to healing the DBRs of either gender or any race. If this were primarily a bw's emotional healing blog, I would put heavy emphasis on DBRbw.

Now you might ask: "Evia, don't you understand that the *issues* of DBRbw contribute to various problems in the black community?" I would answer *yes* to that, but I'd then point out to you that this is not a black community "problems and solutions" blog. Of course, I touch on various pertinent black community topics tangentially, but I always try to keep my blog's important focus in mind. My blog's focus is not to *save alla our people.* I'm not *Superwoman*; I'm a niche worker who focuses on bw's self-care, bettering themselves through making better choices like focusing on health, behaving with decorum, marriage to QLL men, networking with likeminded others, and other commonsense choices. Naturally, this will help the bc to rise but that's a by-product—not my main focus. There is no *one size fits all* for all bw. Some AA women are not ready to hear my particular message. I know that. This is for those who can hear.

Let me also say that many bw out there may have the wherewithal to repair DBRbm, but I'm not one of them. Let me repeat this: I realize that I cannot "repair" DBRbm or DBRbw, so all I try to do with my blog, in that regard, is to warn heterosexual bw who are seeking a mate to *avoid* DBR men, in general.

You might want to read Halima's archives for the whole discussion on DBRs of both genders. This is a forum to generally discuss black women doing what they need to do to 'Live Well'— for those bw who are already capable and determined to do that. Everyone seems to focus on the folks who are totally shattered. What about the ones who have managed to hold themselves together, but still need advice and knowledge about options and alternatives—before they, too, fall apart.

The DBRs are *not* going to live well. Period. I hope my readers are not engaging in magical thinking about that.

Tue Jul 01, 10:32:00 AM EDT 🗑

Spring *said* . . .

Maris, you really said it all and don't ever be afraid to speak your mind when it comes to the horrible things bm say about and do to bw. We have kept quiet for far too long and those days are over. We should no longer allow bm defenders and bm themselves to browbeat us into silence.

Tue Jul 01, 10:42:00 AM EDT 🗑

Spring said...

I don't know if that comment was aimed at me, taking into account our back-and-forth on another blog . . . .

I really don't get this at all. (sigh)

Evia said...

> *However, please believe me we have talked about DBR BW ad nauseam, specifically on Evia's blog.*

Yeah, *Sele*, I have talked about DBRbw and referred to them in various ways and tried to give them info that could help them, but I also realize that some of them are way beyond the scope of my message.

Also, I strongly believe that the vast majority of AA women are not DBRs and most bw who read my blog are ready to 'Live Well,' which includes (for many of them) finding their quality, loving, and lovable man. ☺

Tue Jul 01, 11:05:00 AM EDT 🗑

Evia said...

> *I don't know if that comment was aimed at me, taking into account our back-and-forth on another blog. . .*

I really don't get this at all. (sigh)

I hope y'all understand that the way to stop the "back and forth" is to just show that you are the more mature of the two and just stop it.

I've had to do that—just stop talking to some people because it'll never end, otherwise.

Keep in mind that all of your comments are helping a large

number of people—who read what you write here—to learn and grow, so it'd be a shame if anyone is deprived of any contribution of yours that might be contained in the same comment as a 'back and forth.' But if any more comments about whatever this is about come in, I won't post them.

Tue Jul 01, 11:19:00 AM EDT 🗑

Thisthat said . . .

> *Obama can't stop bw from coddling, enabling, excusing, catering unconditionally to bm which is what contributes to most of the disrespect and disdain heaped on bw by bm.*

I have talked to several bw about filing for child support or checking to see if they can get it increased. You would think I'd put a gun to their heads. Not only do they have to fight bm, but they have to deal with the bm's relatives like the mamas who don't want their sons in jail for non-payment of child support.

One lady was getting $25 per month for her daughter and the guy had a masters degree. She fed her 3 kids hotdogs regularly and left them unsupervised because she could not afford food or childcare and made too much money for assistance. She finally had her support adjusted and their quality of life increased three-fold. Sadly, to this day, she still remains supportive of that bm. Such misguided loyalty.

Tue Jul 01, 11:43:00 AM EDT 🗑

Evia said...

> *Face it—most of us are simply dogs, and black or white, the only thing that changes the fundamental nature of a man is his faith in and trust of God.*

This same topic came up last night at my women's group

and the response from some women was the same: that women need to seek out a "godly man." I don't understand what this term really means because whenever it's defined to me, I can see that it's leaving out a lot of fantastic men.

For ex. my husband is not what some folks would label a "godly man," but when we discussed whether it was prudent to make sex a priority as we developed our relationship, we both agreed that it shouldn't be a priority. Too much was at stake.

There are people who just can't believe as you say:

> . . . *at the end of the day...if you truly LOVE a woman you're going to be willing to wait.*

Exactly! This is such common sense. Some of those same folks who wouldn't think he's a 'godly man' don't believe me when I say that he was willing to wait. They don't seem to think that a man *can* control himself. ☺

> *Real men are leaders who don't wait for women to set a standard. Speaking as a white man, and more importantly just as a man...*

This is *key*. And neither does a "real" man wait for a woman to *let him* be a man. I hear all of this stuff about how 'bw won't *let* a man be a man.' Ludicrous. If I have to *let* a man be a man, then I'm already in charge and feeling like his mommy 'letting' him do something. ☺ I don't respect men of that type and I've always avoided them. My husband is a soft-spoken man, but he's a strong man who knows his own mind and has his own standards. He also has the relationship skills to "persuade" me to agree rather than try to force me to do anything.

> *Let me rephrase it like this, what man can*

claim he loves you if he's willing to compromise and damage your conscience and fill your heart with guilt and fear just because he has 'needs'?

So true. This is so simple, but if you wrote a book with this message, it'd probably be a bestseller these days because so many people have lost contact with normal common sense thinking.

Tue Jul 01, 11:52:00 AM EDT 🗑

Spring said...

Keep in mind that all of your comments are helping a large number of people out there to learn and grow so it'd be a shame if anyone is deprived of any contribution of yours that might be contained in the same comment as a 'back and forth,' but if any more comments about whatever this is about come in, I won't post them.

Thanks Evia. I don't participant in online catfights and I am not here to argue with other bw. How would that be uplifting? However, I will rip disrespectful bm a new one, if I have to. ☺

I really hope anything I have said in my comments haven't offended anyone. I do hope some of my comments have been beneficial to you and the bf posters on this blog and other blogs because I have definitely benefited from yours and theirs. I also will not let anyone stop me from continuing to share my points of view either.

Tue Jul 01, 12:25:00 PM EDT 🗑

ThankfulVisitor said...

I never came across the blog until now and I must say I love the message. This might sound crazy, and maybe I'm asking some of you women who are fighting so hard for the betterment of Black women to do too much, but I hope that it is in your plans to branch out online to different sites and spread the word to bw.

There are a lot of sites frequented by Black people that so many bw frequent too, where they are un-rightfully bashed and they need to not only receive uplifting messages like this but they need to be armed with the words and points that you fabulous women so eloquently come up with to defend themselves. You'd be surprised that a lot of these women don't even realize they are being preyed upon and tricked into doing others' bidding to no advantage for themselves. Please consider visiting some of these sites and preaching your message!

Again, thank you, sistas!

Tue Jul 01, 03:21:00 PM EDT 🗑

Sara said...

Fantastic post, Evia, and welcome back. It's wonderful to hear your voice of reason and logic once again.

Tue Jul 01, 09:14:00 PM EDT 🗑

Evia said...

Hey Sara! Thanks and *thank you* for all you do to continue to open as many eyes as possible about bw's relationships and financial options and free bw from the 'cage,' as Halima puts it.

I hope some of the new folks who come here will definitely check out your slant on this topic. As more bw know better, they will do better which means—make better choices.

All along people have accused bloggers like me and you of trying to get bw to run into the arms of wm, whereas the fact is that I have tried to get bw to make "better" choices irrespective of the skin shade of the man. Bw must position themselves to do that and this re-positioning process is primarily mental because thoughts precede actions.

When a woman is on a quest to survive, thrive, and Live Well, a shrewd woman puts her own interests *first and foremost*' (subtitle of my first book) and knows that the skin shade of her loving and lovable man of *quality* is irrelevant. Some other groups of women *know* this and operate with this in mind because they were taught this. I was taught that *quality* is the absolutely most critical factor in choosing a man.

Many people overlook the importance of this *teaching* factor, but I've now seen the need to share what I know with bw, and this is why I now refer to my blogs as *'teaching essays.'*

Most bw are still being taught or indoctrinated with the same old played-out info that has failed bw. Not many of them are going to come out winners with that old info. They are being dumbed-down, and it doesn't occur to them to wonder or question why the teachers of these teachings are doing so bad themselves.

Wed Jul 02, 09:36:00 AM EDT 🗑

PVW said...

Welcome back, Evia! I like the *magical thinking* argument. I describe it as: "Real world women don't live their lives based upon hopeful fantasies!"

Hoping, fantasizing instead of doing what has to be done in the "real world" is just too crazy, and it is not what "real" women do!

Wed Jul 02, 09:50:00 AM EDT 🗑

Sherry said...

I have a slightly different outlook on the "magical thinking." I actually think it could work very well for BW *if* they look to Michelle Obama. BW and young girls (my focus) will have their beliefs about *self* greatly bolstered by seeing a woman like her as the First Lady, because they will begin to understand the power we have when we make thoughtful, forward-thinking life decisions, and school ourselves continuously and consciously.

Evia has always advocated putting ourselves first, and that is something I always believed in. When I do this, I am sometimes told I am "selfish" by people outside my family. Lol. And by the way, my "selfish" behaviour usually meant that *they* could not achieve something because I was not "assisting" them, as though that were my duty and obligation. I don't think so!

Where the magical thinking should come into play positively for us, is when we remove unsuitable men from the equation, and think of ourselves, and what *we each* wish to accomplish in life.

Since we are not God, we cannot "wish and hope" that others will be inspired to better their lives. We can only "magically think" and do for us, and I absolutely believe it is a palpable power that we are able to manifest and use for betterment in our lives. When the bar is set high, you automatically adjust your steps accordingly.

So be selfish. You cannot help anyone else until you help yourselves first anyway (for those who have problems with labeling themselves as selfish).

Wed Jul 02, 12:45:00 PM EDT 🗑

Maris said...

> *You really said it all and don't ever be afraid to speak your mind when it comes to the horrible things bm say about and do to bw. We have kept quiet for far too long and those days are over. We should no longer allow bm defenders and bm themselves to browbeat us into silence.*

Thank you for your kind words, Spring. I really feel like saying this: I understand now that we passively, but surely, cooperate when we remain silent. That's one big lesson I've learned from reading BW-IR blogs.

I'm just starting to be vocal about these issues, and I share this information with my girlfriends, I'm so grateful for these blogs! I've got a few negative reactions (un-doing what the BC-Indoctrination has done is a process that I went thru as well, so I understand the hostility), but some very positive ones as well. Once I realized I had been "conditioned to defend and excuse BM "no matter what" and admitted this was an unhealthy habit I needed to put an end to—to preserve my sanity and overall well-being—my emotional state changed in a very drastic way.

I feel *free* today. I used to be loyal because I believed what I had been taught, and also out of fear. But these blogs, Halima's, Sara's, Evia's, CW's, and etc., made me realize one thing about DBRbm: They treat us as mere *options* while we BW make them our *top priority*. That's why I decided my *top* priority will be *me* from now on.

When it comes to being your number #1 priority, the example of *J-Lo* comes to mind. When she left *Puffy* during the case with rapper *SHYNE*, people called her all the names in the book. If there's one thing J-Lo did in her life that I respect, it has to be her leaving Puffy. Instead of staying with an unstable, unfaithful man with multiple kids from different women, all in the name of *loyalty*, J-Lo chose J-Lo's interests, J-Lo's peace of mind first of all, J-Lo's safety, J-Lo's quality life, J-Lo's career, J-Lo's endorsements, and J-Lo's other business ventures. In other words, J-Lo chose J-LO! Love her or hate her, she did the right thing. Even if she had feelings for him, she chose "her" over being that man's option. When you look at Kim Porter's situation, can you blame J-Lo?

BW's top priority should be BW—*your* interests and *your* well-being. And if that doesn't please others, bleep them! Who sacrifices for *you* and treats you as a *top priority* in the BC??
Thu Jul 03, 01:48:00 PM EDT 🗑

Meryl said...

Maris, you hit it dead on! You can choose to be like J-Lo (no matter what anyone thinks of her talents, etc.). Or you can be a glorified baby-mama on the cover of Essence and still ain't—yes AIN'T ☺—one step closer to that altar. J-Lo has been married now for umm 5 years, I think, with twins. And let's examine where his other women are?
Thu Jul 03, 06:08:00 PM EDT 🗑

Yvette said...

> Maybe, I just don't understand how bw (and other women too) can "love" all of these unworthy men! I can understand why the mamas of these guys would love their sons, but puhlease! I mean, what are these guys bringing to the table . . . .

A friend and I had this discussion earlier today. We were

saying how sorry we feel for black women who just don't get it!

Evia, your blog is such a valuable tool for black women.

Thu Jul 03, 09:56:00 PM EDT 🗑

Yvette said...

> *You wait until she gets into the White House. Black women are going to be in so much demand, the BC will be bawling. If you think that the BM and other BC complaining about us now, you wait until November 2008, when Barack is elected.*

Very true. I have heard her called "*attractive*" and I have heard her called "homely." The people who called her attractive were white. The people who called her homely were black men—of course.

Thu Jul 03, 10:10:00 PM EDT 🗑

Maris said...

EXACTLY, Meryl!

Fri Jul 04, 02:08:00 AM EDT 🗑

Lena said...

First of all Evia, I hope it wasn't coming across as a back-and-forth as I only made one comment to the poster. I have been coming to your site long before the whole thing started (DBR, Mammy, bm-bashing accusations), and I did not really agree with a lot of the things that were said about you. I have never felt the need to defend any bm. It may have something to do with me being Nigerian, so I'm used to being in a country that is predominantly black. Hence, when a black man screws up, I say he screwed up.

However, I didn't want sisters on this site to think all black women were *for* them. There are some that no matter what, will defend the most despicable bm to death, and even criticise the bm doing good, 'cuz in their heads, it's the 'right' thing to do. Black women (or at least the sensible ones) should surround themselves with positive people and keep away from negative people of whichever gender or group.

We have been so used to seeing negative as *white* and positive as *black*, that even though most of our attackers are now black (males), we still cannot separate ourselves. And even some of those that have realised that the devil can come in black skin (just as he can come in white), are yet to realise that he can also come as a female (even if she is black). The fact that one is a black woman should not lead anyone to think that all other black women would look out for her.

Sat Jul 05, 12:21:00 AM EDT 🗑

Lena said...

> *You wait until she gets into the White House. Black women are going to be in so much demand, the BC will be bawling. . . .*

That is only so true. If it is a bw like Michelle, that certainly would improve bw's image. It would lift up bw who are more like her, i.e. ones with a more classy demeanor and persona. I hope young black girls (and even grown women) see her and realise this is how to behave. Dignified. They have tried to pin the whole 'angry black woman' thing on her but can't. Black women can look at Michelle and realise that we don't have to live up to any stereotype that others have created for us.

She is now a style icon. I will also admit she is one of the reasons I like Barack. Taking on his policies, she is sort of the icing on the cake. However, I really hope she will use her influence to real effect, not only worldwide, but particularly in the 'AA community'. Little AA girls need to see who she really is and realise that they, too, deserve better than what might be forced on them by those in the 'community'.

Sat Jul 05, 12:27:00 AM EDT 🗑

Mistyel said...

Evia, thank you for such an insightful, candid and well thought post! I so admire you and your determination to make other Black women see that they we are worthy of being loved, cared for and respected.

Kudos to you! You are still my *shero*!

Sun Jul 06, 04:20:00 PM EDT 🗑

Anonymous said...

No! Don't date white men. Date within your race! ☺ Just kidding. As an African-American man, I think a congrats is in order. I think that it is wonderful that all of you are opening yourselves to new and exciting people that will make you that perfect partner. I only ask that you'd teach bw not to be bitter toward any group of people and teach them of their history—not only from your husband's side, but also your side as well.

For all that aren't doing this to get back at some of our brothers out there, a special congrats to you and your family. I know that house will be full of love and support.

Wed Jul 23, 11:10:00 PM EDT

7

Some Men are Just Special

July 20, 2006

Ah, I'm still a little drowsy from last night's long drive back from D.C. We went to see the performance of *3 Mo' Divas* at the Arena Stage there. If you can make it there to see the show, or if it comes to your area, see it! Vivian Reed's performance will be one of the best you will ever see. Trust me. She is a true *diva*, meaning her talent is unearthly, which is the true meaning of the word "*diva*." The other two divas—one is a bw—were also great, but Vivian stole the show.

My IR couple radar picked up one other IR couple—a black guy with an Asian woman. They sat next to us. There were a bunch of bw there with black men and as usual, there were lots of bw there either alone or with other women.

Anyway, my husband's birthday is coming up, so it was a birthday treat from me to him. With us, treats are special things—sometimes unusual things—we do for each other or give each other. We give each other multiple treats on each others' birthday and other days like Valentine's day (we go overboard), Mother's day (he treats me), and though we don't believe in the commercialism surrounding Christmas, we use it as an *excuse* to give each other more treats. This is just one of the ways we express our deep appreciation and love for each other.

As I think I mentioned before, he also likes to surprise me even at other times by doing things for me or giving me little things that he knows I want or will like. He is a true *romantic* and makes our relationship a priority. That's just natural for him. He's just a special man, a loving mate.

This has nothing to do with his race. My ex-husband (a black man) was also a rare find. There are some really fantastic guys out there, but you have to lower your guard and be receptive to them. Don't cross any man off the list due to his race, ethnicity, and other superficial factors alone. Just screen men carefully for the really important qualities.

I might add that even though my ex-husband is black, some AAs considered him unsuitable because he was born and bred in Africa. Well, I guess you've figured out by now, I don't allow *other peoples' opinions* stop me from doing what's best for me. Posted by Evia at **7/20/2006 08:48:00 AM**

On the Verge of Losing the "Black Woman Card"

February 6, 2008

[Picture on SITE of black woman-white man couple: Pamela J. Joyner, socialite and co-chair of the San Francisco Ballet and Founding Partner of Avid Partners, LLC & Husband, Fred Giuffrida, managing director of funds, Horsley Bridge Partners, (Silicon Valley)]

The bw in the pic above is a definite violator of the "black woman code." Her *black card* has been canceled in many black circles. Imagine co-chairing the San Francisco Ballet *and* marrying a white man! Major "black woman" points, she's lost— right there. OMG! She's lost so many points until the *black police* will never give her card back.

I was thinking yesterday about how so much of the criticism about me from other black folks throughout my life has come about because they don't think I behave like a *black* woman. I was considered a bw who had left the group and was viewed as something akin to a *'sell-out'* long before I married Darren. Yep. I almost lost my "black" card years ago when I married my African ex-husband and packed up everything and moved to Nigeria with him to live forever and ever. That was proof positive to my southern relatives and even most of my NY friends and acquaintances that I *had forgotten where I came from.* Some said I thought I was *too good* for a home-grown AA man.

My relatives reasoned with me, tried to get me to change my mind, and warned me not to go with him for about a year before we shipped all of our belongings to Nigeria. When they saw that I was determined to go "over there" as they termed it, they said their goodbyes with an air of resignation that said they'd done all they could to save me from myself. (smh)

They never expected for me to survive, *over there.* Actually, my relatives were surprised that I had survived my college years in NYC—but moving to Africa was like going to another planet to them. Going to the moon would have been more understandable to them. At least, they'd watched people go to the moon on TV. To them, going to Africa was something that *crazy white folks* did but African-American women were supposed to have the good sense to go to church regularly, get an education, get married to a home-grown black man, have kids, get a good job, and stay safely in the U.S.A. ☺

I considered these folks to be seriously underexposed! It never seems to occur to most underexposed AAs, even now, that black women (including many African-American women) are all over the world doing all kinds of things, living lives that they only see here in glitzy movies and glossy magazines—doing practically everything they want in some cases *and* being loved, cherished, and adored by men who are quality, loving, and lovable men. LOL!

In general, when AAs typically think or say that black women *do* or *don't do* this or that, they're not thinking/talking about a black woman from Lesotho, Rio, or Kingston; they're talking about a black American woman. Likewise, when an AA woman makes the declaration: "I'm a *'black' woman*," she's packing a lot into that label. She's declaring she's different from other women. In essence, she's *othering* herself.

"Black" in this context carries with it, a script, and its parameters are always very limiting, confining, and often suffocating for that woman. Usually, there are only short-ranged benefits, if any at all for her, but loads of benefits for the black community at large. This is why a black woman can be praised as hardworking and generous to a fault by those in the bc, but that woman often lives an empty, lonely, sad, financially and socially impoverished personal life. There is virtually no reciprocity from others in the typical black community.

However, many bw adhere closely to this script, expertly learn and perform their part, and even monitor other bw to make sure that others of their gender learn and stick to the script. Black women in the U.S. are ever vigilant about this because apparently no "black" woman here wants to suffocate all by herself. LOL!

If a bw does not stick to the script, she is frequently chided, confronted in direct and indirect ways, ridiculed, and even ostracized—for ex., not included in the chat circuit with other bw, or other social activities. If she doesn't slide back into place, she's usually talked about extremely negatively—sometimes vilified, and eventually put on the "out" list.

Rarely will other bw speak up for her, or if they do, they can easily be persuaded to back down because they, too, fear being put on the *out* list. After all, she has broken the "black girl/woman's" code and many bw earn brownie points from bm and the bc in general by becoming code *enforcers*. This code exists to control the black girl/woman's behavior, time, energy, money, talents, skills, abilities, sexuality, and overall resources in order to keep AA women working for the *'cause,'* fighting the *'good fight'* to uplift the black community.

AA men, in general, are not held responsible to work for the *cause, so* there is barely any pressure on them to fight the *good fight*. This is complete role reversal because it's the *men* in other groups who confront and fight, not women. AA women are indoctrinated from a young age to become the front line soldiers or so-called *sista soldiers*, fighting the good fight all *alone*.

The bulk of AA girls learns at a young age to adhere to this script/code or at least try not to get caught if they do deviate from it.

If you're an AA female, I'm sure you can think of 10 things in 10 seconds that black girls/women "don't do"—if you're really "black" or have ever been a card-carrying *black woman*. ☹ And the "black" police are always out looking for violators. For ex., a friend of mine was saying she hates to hear black teenage girls talk like 'Valley' girls. When I asked her why, she explained that this is talking like white girls. *Black girls don't do that; they need to just talk like "black" girls.*

I dropped the subject with her right there because I knew exactly where that was going, and I get tired of trying to enlighten black folks about how they strangle themselves and each other. They then blame whites for keeping them down. Too sad! Besides, she wouldn't have been able to explain the way "black" girls are *supposed* to talk. She would have tried but would have gotten frustrated and ended with "*you know what I mean.*"☺

Regarding IR dating and relationships, one of the things that most black girls/women *don't do* is flirt with wm when there are black people around or usually not at all. There is still lots of direct and subtle pressure put on bw and black teenage girls to just wait for their black 'Mr. Right.' In the black area near where I live, there is still pressure put on the teenage black girls to avoid, ignore, or behave coldly towards white boys/men or white-skinned men.

For ex, there is a very pleasant, young, college-graduated wm who is a member of my predominantly black church. He's tall, good-looking, and well educated at a top-rated university. I would definitely be interested in him if I were single and in that age range. LOL! I've noticed that none of the young black women at the church will even look in his direction. Instead, when there's socializing after the church service, they chase after the young DBRbm there—most of whom have one or more girlfriends who are either biracial or Hispanic.

Anyway, on Sunday, maybe I'll directly ask some of these

young women why they're not paying this white guy any attention. I can tell he's ripe for the picking. After all, he joined a black church and attends more regularly than most bm. Some of the bw may be very interested in this white guy, but I already know it would go against the bw's code for them to sit near him or smile at him directly or chitchat with him. They know it's a code violation too. They'd be scolded and may get their bw's card yanked. However, this is exactly why so many of these young bw end up unmarried and babymamas. The men they like and chase after will most often not marry them.

Most AA women still hesitate to say or absolutely won't say to any black person they know that they find some wm attractive. This is definitely against the black girl/woman's code. I continue to get stoic, face-tightening looks from some blacks in public when I'm laughing at something my husband says to me when we're out having a good time. A bw is not *supposed* to enjoy being with a wm.

There is a long list of '*don't-dos with or around' wm* for "black" women in the U.S.

All of these don't-dos with wm prevent some black females from relating normally to a white man in a situation when she meets an interested, quality wm or any white-skinned man. I get lots of private notes from black women, and a major theme in many of the notes is a variety of questions related to how to behave around wm or what to expect from wm. Likewise, I often get notes from wm expressing their hesitancy around bw. Neither group feels comfortable just being *natural* with the other. Of course, this does not apply to *all* individuals in either of these groups, obviously, or none of us would have connected and married.

By the time I started dating wm, I didn't feel any more uncomfortable around wm than I felt about a typical "new" bm because I always knew that *all* men had to be evaluated carefully or *vetted*. I knew that each type of man came with a warning label, so I never gave *any* new man a free pass. I didn't care how a wm thought about me in the deep recesses of his brain; I cared about the way he *treated* me. This is the same way I regard *any* man, and I remove myself from any man's life if he disrespects me or mistreats me. So I didn't have any concern about a wm mistreating me. I knew he could only do that if I gave him the opportunity. Therefore, I was a carefree, equal-opportunity dater who vetted *all* men.

After blogging for years now and reading hundreds of email notes and comments from other AA women who have swallowed massive doses of the typical bw's *indoctrination* program, I have to say that I now realize that I escaped mostly all the indoctrination or was immune to it. If not, I too would have been very uncomfortable around wm and wouldn't have included them in my romantic mate pool. I, too, would have been a sista-soldier who avoided white men romantically or greeted them all with a snarl.

Many AA women don't think that wm find them attractive and worthwhile because the indoctrination from the DBR crew and other spirit-crushing elements in the bc constantly tell them that the *only* men who will find a bw attractive or think highly of them is a bm. If I'd doubted my attractiveness and worth to a wm, I would have behaved very differently when Darren expressed interest in me. I would have been suspicious of his motives and probably would have responded in a negative way. I would have probably suspected he was a fetishist or worse.

However, I did not doubt my attractiveness and worth to any man, so I saw him as a man who was interested in me—a woman. If my black *flavor* made me more appealing to him, I saw that as a plus. I knew we'd have to talk about society's racial issues, but initially, that wasn't a point of concern for me. If he was earnest, I believed we could handle that.

Racial and ethnic differences have never been an issue for me when I relate to men or women. Darren and I talk about racial issues sometimes, and bluntly. We both agree that the race *construct* is mainly a tool for manipulating all the "races" and privileging whites.

AA women need to forget about this bw script/code and just be women when they're around appealing men of quality. As a matter of fact, any bw who wants to meet quality men tonight should just go to where you think men of this type are in any part of town and adopt the script of a lighthearted, friendly woman. It gets easier over time, as everything does. Go to these places often.

The time has come for AA women to stop trying to behave like a "black" woman and just be a woman. Trying to "act black" or "talk black" and continuing to act like the loyal black woman *sista soldier* who is hell-bent on saving black people is a lose-lose stratagem and very unfeminine. Men, in general, including black men, do *not* want a long-term committed relationship with an unfriendly, battle-worn, angry sista soldier, fighting against white hegemony. That robs her of her femininity.

I've even wondered why it is so many black people in the U.S. *cling* to the "black" label when it's a label stemming from an evil construct (racism, the 1-drop rule) that ushered forth so much death and destruction for black people here. I think they cling to it because they have no other *identity*.

I would ask any AA women to think about what she personally gains from being a *black* woman. This label requires her to adhere to the very narrow, limiting, constricting "black" woman script/code. It's impossible to keep the label without sticking to the code because other blacks monitor bw's behavior and are always ready to pounce when a bw deviates from the bw's code.

So, bw, I would suggest that you compare the gains from your current code adherence compare to what you could gain if you just took on the role of a friendly, unburdened, *feminine* woman. Period. You should, of course, expect for other AAs to call you a *sell-out* or blast you for *acting like a white woman,* and try to snap you back into the role of the angry, *sista soldier-shemale* AA woman. But think about it; being called names is a very small price to pay for freedom.

I know so many AA women *sista soldiers* because most AA women think that's how they're supposed to act. That's their *identity.* They consider themselves *saviors.* Their indoctrination has caused them to marry that role. They never ask themselves what they've personally gained from performing that role, or whether it's enough. They never think about *reciprocity.*

We all should try a new role sometimes. Try the role of the friendly bw when interacting with men who appear to be of quality. I can virtually predict that you will meet more people and have many more fulfilling interactions with men.

The 'black woman's code' is an obsolete code. It's an anti-life code for most upwardly mobile AA women at this point because it is not enabling these women to find quality mates with whom they can create viable, long lasting relationships. Many black women in the upwardly mobile category are therefore opting to have no children or mate and reproduce with partners who are not emotionally and financially committed to them or their children. This usually puts the children at risk of never developing their potential and pushes the black mother into a life of struggling all alone with the children.

This lonely struggle also forces her to de-prioritize her own self-care and neglect her femininity and health, which results in fewer chances to mate with quality men. It also frequently results in poverty. Single bw with children continue to be the poorest demographic in the country.

I proudly declare myself a staunch violator of the "black" woman code, and I have a loving husband, well-adjusted and successful children, a comfortable lifestyle, and a network of supportive people in my life to show for it. The "black" police yanked my "black" woman's card a long time ago. That actually became 'the wind beneath my wings.' I'm so grateful to them because they helped me to soar.

9

What's Done in the Dark

July 22, 2006

I've been predicting that bw's interracial relationships are going to grow by leaps and bounds. Many black people in the United States, however, are just not prepared emotionally for this.

The fact is that interracial relationships have *always* occurred throughout history and throughout the world. It is understandable, given the United States' history of chattel slavery, that so many black people think that American whites and blacks ought not to be interested in interracial mating with each other. However, if people could be dissuaded from or kept from mating with each other based on historical conflict between them, there would be very little mating because there has been strife between the vast majority of groups at some point in history.

Women and men of all races are human beings with innate, hard-wired sexual drives. The sex drive is an extremely strong God-given drive, thus much stronger than the mere fabricated, social, and evil construction of "race." Keep in mind, we were human *before* we were "black" and "white" because *black* and *white* are political constructs.

Added to this, humans have complex make-ups that cause us to seek out compatible others. Given the differences in population between whites and blacks and given the intermixing in schools and workplaces, etc., this means that there can be many white women, for ex. in a given area, who are more compatible with an individual black man in that area than I would be for that black man. And likewise, there can be many white men, in a given area, who are more compatible with a given black woman than she'd be with any black man in that area. If these people from different races meet and are attracted to and receptive to each other, then you have an interracial couple.

A key element to understanding this compatibility issue is that even though my husband and I wear the skin *labels* of black and white, we are so much more than our label. My skin label of *black*—even *if* much what it implies is true of me—is just one element of my being. My skin shade appeals to my husband, but he mostly appreciates the many other aspects of me, as I appreciate his qualities and traits. It is those other aspects that make us compatible and our relationship a fulfilling one.

Unfortunately, when some people see us together, they filter us through their warped thought system to focus *only* on our skin labels. So they ask, "What do that *white* man and *black* woman see in each other?" Or they quickly judge us negatively or inaccurately, or both. Furthermore, whites and blacks never get a chance to openly discuss or work through their feelings due to fear of what could happen (maybe, confrontation) if whites and blacks freely talk about the varying residues of stress in both groups that is related to slavery, Jim Crow, and the present-day structured racism in American society.

It's common to hear American blacks mutter, *"How can all of this interracial stuff be happening?"* as if this is something new.☺ This is a form of self-delusion that author, Halima Anderson—who published a book encouraging black women to explore interracial relationships as a way to expand their dating pool—examines in one of her enlightening posts at her website: *http://dateawhiteguy.blogspot.com.*

Let's recall that miscegenation (white racial purity) laws were surely *not* passed during slavery in the U.S. to stop blacks from pursuing whites as mates. There were many other harsh, punitive measures to control black impulses in this regard. White men created those laws and vigorously enforced them to prevent other white men from *openly* having relationships with and *marrying* black women during slavery. This extended into the days of Jim Crow and afterwards. If a sizeable number of white men had not been trying to do that, laws would not have been necessary to ban it.

Widespread racial admixture that's apparent in the

bloodlines of African-Americans show that these laws certainly didn't stop large numbers of white men from having sex (forcibly so, in many cases) with black women. Various accounts of history also show that some white women had a sexual interest in black men.

My point is that people have sexual/romantic interest in each other. Humans are innately wired in this manner. This will always exist, and even with laws, sanctions, severe penalties, and sometimes death, many of these people, despite having different skin labels, will act on this interest. This is because there are no essential differences between *races* of people.

10

Living Well is the Best Success—Best Revenge

August 17, 2006

I want to respond to some provocative excerpts from a post from commenter, Ann.

Ann said:

"Would your husband be interested in doing a post once a week on his takes on things?

The reason I ask this is because, as you know, many black women have fears of going into any kind of relationship with a white man, especially when the sex issue comes up. Granted our fears are justified with the brutal mistreatment of white men during slavery, the inhumane continuation of this horror during Jim Crow/segregation (and remember, segregation only ended a mere 40 years ago), American society still, in 2006, shows its contempt towards black women in the media, TV, newsprint, and ads in many negative images, and so on. Why must black women be made to feel as if we are the ones to make the first move, especially where white men are concerned?

We are the ones who come from a history of being sexually brutalized, just based on our race and color alone. Not white women. Not Asian women. Not Latino women. Not Native American women. Black women only.

We are a race of women who for over 350 YEARS have been treated in ways worse than a prostitute should be treated. And many white men expect black women to just "mosey" up to them like yesterday not only didn't happen, but also to act as if the legacy of white men's cruel treatment of us has not left a bitter, fearful distrust of them? The aftereffects of that legacy are still with us to this day.

Many white men have a hard time "getting next" to black women because many refuse to learn their history—-America's history of vicious hateful treatment of black women and girls. And as we can see, everyone knows of black men's history: Jim Crow, sharecropping, denial of employment they were well qualified for in the South, hideous lynchings.

But, say something to people about black women's history in America, and you get blank stares or incredulous looks: "What! Black women were gang-raped during slavery? Black women were still raped over 100+ years way after slavery ended? What! Black women are women?

Goes back to what I always say (but mostly privately think)

about peoples' perceived images of blacks/women in America:
"All the Blacks are Men; All the Women are White; But, Some of
Us are Brave."

So, you see what I am trying to say, Evia, is that many
white men do not know of our history in America, but we know
of their history in America. Of course, I am not crazy enough to
expect white people to truly learn of all the many cruel and
hateful things done by their race to ours. That would be living in
dreamland."

Ann, I understand, but I want you to realize that *all* bw
don't feel your level of trauma. Some of us feel none of that and
others who may have felt some of it have worked through it.
Growth comes from working through episodes from the past
that are harming us in the present. That's a big burden you're
carrying. Who is it hurting? Who is it weighing down? You can't
change the past. Whew! You can't live well in the present if
you're carrying that kind of burden. What would it take to get
you to lay down that burden?

I don't think that white men *expect* black women to "mosey
up" to them or make the first move. My husband made the first
move; I was simply receptive to his advances. He didn't do any
of those brutal acts that you mentioned, so I was *not* fearful of
him because he couldn't do anything to me, in the *present* that I
didn't allow him to do. I'm not stuck in the past. I also don't
trust *any* man with my heart, unless he proves himself to be
worthy.

I think that you're seeing *all* white men as rapists and
brutalizers of black women. That's convenient, but they didn't

and don't *all* perpetrate or condone the injustices. We know from the historical record that some decent whites *opposed* slavery and Jim Crow with their words and their actions, but they didn't have the power (guns) to stop what was happening. There was a ton of money in the practice of slavery and white privileges are very valuable to a lot of whites. It would have taken a massive army to eradicate slavery or white privileges during Jim Crow. If we look at both racism and sexism, the majority of whites and men (black men, included) are not going to work hard to eradicate a system that benefits them.

Slavery was a money-making machine similar to drug trafficking these days. Why don't you or I and other decent ones of us stop the drug traffickers from killing and destroying the lives of tons of others? It's because we don't have the power (army). If we try to stand up to the big drug cartels, we'll be squashed instantly. Would *you* want the numerous victims of drug traffickers to hold *you*, as an individual, responsible in the future for not stopping the drug trade that brutalizes them and their families?

Many white men *do* know the history of this country even better than many blacks, but knowing the history doesn't *change* the history. My husband certainly knows the history, but he cannot change it, and I don't hold him responsible for what racist whites did then or do now. Whenever he can, he does oppose injustices.

Regarding my husband writing a post in my blog, well, he has his own activities. My blog is not of interest to him. If you want to have a dialogue with a white man about any issue, there are plenty of them online, if nowhere else, who apparently are very involved in just about any message board or mailing list on any topic.

Interested white men are a large group of men that some black women *may* choose to add to their dating pool. If you are unable to regard an individual white man without remembering that men with his skin shade raped and brutalized black women, then IMO, it would not be healthy for you to even consider dating a white man. *Why are you even thinking about it?*

Ann, the fact is that many white men, black men, white women, Asian women, Hispanic women, and others have greatly enlarged their dating pool, and they seem quite happy with the results. I do understand that they don't have our history. However, it's AA women (and similar bw in other places) who are the *most* unhappy about *their* present dating or marriage prospects, *not* white men.

You should work through your fear and anger towards present-day white men, primarily for your own good. Otherwise, you'll just be stuck with the anger because nothing you do today can change the past. The only thing you can do now is to change the way you think about the past.

I think that AA women need to decide—whether to remain stuck in history that none of us can change or to focus fully on thriving *today*. That's what my ancestors would want. That would be the absolute best way to honor them and make their struggles worthwhile.

If a black woman decides that dwelling on history will enhance her ability to survive and thrive *today*, then I would suggest that she does that. I believe, however, that those among my ancestors who perished or were diminished in any way at the hands of white brutalizers would advise me, *"Stewing in anger is for losers. Take your cards and play them well so that you can come out on top!"* which actually means to "live well." Can the typical AA woman 'live well' by restricting herself to 'nothing but a black man'? The numbers don't support that. Look around you. Be realistic and answer that. Also, *some* black men— especially many AA men—have *shown* that black women are the women, they value the least.

I agree with those who say that *'Living well is the best revenge'*. I've never thought about any revenge, but I *do* live well. A significant part of that is due to my husband who enables me to live a laid-back, contented life. It's not about his *supposed* money; it's about his qualities and traits, the man he is, and his putting various kinds of action behind how he says he feels about me. When a man says he's committed to you or loves you, he ought to *show* it. That's what my husband does.

So I figure that if I have this life, then other bw might be interested in having it too. It's an option—not a requirement. No one is forcing this on any bw. You have free will. Each woman largely chooses her fate.

White men are simply the largest group of available men to AA women in this country, aside from AA men. For those who advocate that black women date and marry black men from other countries (interculturally, as I did), then I wholeheartedly agree with that option also because that worked for me, but that will not put a dent in the large number of marriage-seeking AA women who are unable to find suitable mates. White men are plentiful, and many of them are interested. They just *are*.

COMMENTS:

JJ said...

You know, I have one friend who objects to dating white men because of similar reasons to Ann's.

I have another friend who has started the internet-dating thing and has become a bit discouraged by the profiles that list every ethnicity *except* 'Black' as a possibility to date—even from black men! One black guy's profile said, "Only White Women Need Respond."

So I think a (purely anecdotal) number of Black women don't feel like white men are going to find them attractive or desirable and how are you able to distinguish between the white guy who is genuinely interested and the one who is just after sex.

My personal feeling is, that is a problem that can be an issue with any man, although heightened with a white man because you know the stereotypes that are out there about Black women.

How do you convince *some* black women that *all* white men aren't out to use them? Or mistreat them, etc.

Personally, my *objection* to white men doesn't stem from any sort of history, or even fear of someone being interested in only sex; it boils down to attraction. Plain and simple. That, and I must admit, I find *some* white guys lame, boring, dull and a tad effeminate. Sorry, I know that's sad but true. Dammit, if we go to a concert, I expect you to bob your head. Lol.

Seriously, getting past physical attraction is difficult. It's not the end all-be all, but if you can't muster up any "ooh wee" feelings, how do you get to the next step?

Thu Aug 17, 09:01:00 PM EDT

Evia said... re:

> *I have another friend who has started the internet-dating thing and has become a bit discouraged by the profiles that list every ethnicity except Black as a possibility to date.*

People find ways to validate what they already think. You might remind her that many bw *do* meet QLL wm for love and marriage on those sites. I'll bet I could find at least three white guys who do not cross quality black women off the list for each one who does. Let me repeat: If some bw aren't interested in exploring all of their dating and marriage options, that's *their* choice. I think that some black women are simply looking for rejection, and then use any that they find as a reason not to date out—because they *fear* doing it. Ann made that clear.

Dating out is an *option*—not a requirement.

I also have met black women who don't think that white men will find them attractive. Once again, they're projecting *their own feelings* about their attractiveness or lack of it onto white men. One of the problems here is that many black women have never had conversations with white men about the attractiveness or appeal of black women, so these bw are imagining the worst when that's not the case.

Most, if not *all*, men want sex immediately, as you suspect, so of course, white men *are* after sex, but just because they want it doesn't mean a bw has to give it up! That makes it sound like the woman doesn't have self-control.

If that is her concern, this is why a woman should keep her legs closed until enough time has passed, and she's gotten to know the man better—whether he's black, white, or in-between—and he's gotten to know her. I would think that a man who is *only* after sex is not going to spend time with a woman week after week, month after month waiting for sex when sex is so readily available out there.

Honestly, I think that if some bw are so suspicious about what white men want and will allow *any* man to take charge of them and their body without screening him first, those women should not be out there mingling with men at all because they will be taken advantage of by one man or another—sooner rather than later.

It's really a shame that women (in all groups) don't exercise more control than this because a woman has a lot of power in a relationship, but unfortunately, some of them don't know this or don't know how to use the clout she has.

I, personally, have never been suspicious about whether any man wanted sex from me. I already knew that because men are pretty easy to read. So I always looked at whether he could offer me what I wanted in a relationship. If he appeared to bring enough of what I wanted to the table, he could at least get my attention. If not, I didn't care what he wanted because he was not the one for me, and I would let him know that quickly because I never wanted to waste a man's time. Likewise, I never allowed a man to waste my time. In the mating realm, *time* is precious for a woman. No woman can afford to waste time!

So, if a bw thinks or believes that the typical white men is out to use her or mistreat her, and feel helpless to prevent it, then IMO it's best that she not date white men because this fear most likely will become a self-fulfilling prophecy.

Insofar as the reasons you cite for your lack of attraction to white men, let's look at this more broadly. Yes, this is true about *some* of them, but not many others. How many wm have you dated or been with at music venues? Do you go to music venues where there are *mostly* white men? How often?

Some men—of *all* groups—are what you call *boring* or *effeminate,* and I'm assuming I understand what you mean by those terms. Some people consider a quiet person to be boring, whereas the person may be a very interesting person who simply doesn't talk much. Some people consider a heterosexual man who displays good manners, cooks well, and cleans the house to be *effeminate.* IMO, that's narrow-minded, stereotypical thinking. Not saying you think that way.

I've often heard bw complain that their bm partner won't dance when they go out. I've been to many music and dancing venues where there were more than a few white men dancing and *'getting down'* ☺ because I go to places with Darren where there are *mostly* white men.

And just because a man bobs his head to music or dances well, that doesn't have anything whatsoever to do with his being a good mate. That's a very insignificant and narrow vetting lens to view a man's marriage and fatherhood qualities and traits through. As I've said many times before, I think that AA women, in general, need a totally different mindset about vetting men for serious relationships. And until a large number of them actually acquire the *correct* vetting lens, they really ought not to shoot themselves and other bw in the foot by crossing off *most* of the men in their environment or proclaiming to these men they are not wanted. Is that smart?

You have to decide what's *most* important to you in a mate because you are most likely not going to be able to get everything you want. There's a whole group of *good time guys* (from the so-called 'party animal' group) out there who usually make lousy mates and fathers. We know that. Yes, it would be great to get everything we ever dreamed of in a mate all rolled into one package, but that's usually just a dream. Getting those traits and qualities that are *most* important to you is the key.

Mature, marriage-minded women face reality and choose loving and lovable men who meet the most important criteria for relationship/marriage success. Many of the wm who some bw might consider lame and boring are actually fun to be with, if you get to know them.

In terms of the *ooh wee* stuff, I was attracted to my husband physically and mentally. He'll never win a *dance fever* contest, but he knew how to get my attention, and he knows how to keep me humming in the *ooh wee* department.☺ So I didn't have to "muster up" *ooh wee* feelings.

How many bw would even allow themselves the opportunity to just spend time relaxing or socializing with white men in the first place—really getting to know them as individual men and vice versa? We know that most bw don't give wm a chance to show other aspects of their personalities. If he doesn't instantly *razzle-dazzle* them and make their heads buzz by talking a bunch of jive nonsense to them (like they're used to some AA men doing), a typical bw from a certain background might think the sincere white guy is *lame*, but that's because she's viewing him through the narrow lens of her cultural background.

My husband never tried to make my head buzz with *talk*; he razzled-dazzled me with his *actions*. After I'd spent more time with him, I discovered he also has a razor wit, which I love, and has a great sense of humor.

Some of us are going to do fine. Some of us are already doing fine in life and love, and living well. However, if AA women, as a group, are going to succeed in the global village on various fronts, they're going to need to be much more *broadminded*. They desperately need a *different thought system*.

And I tell you, *some* white guys have got some *sho nuff* "skills" in the *ooh wee* department! ☺ I mean, in my experience, though limited, and also based on what I've heard, they tend to do whatever it takes to make sure that a woman has her *ooh wee* moments! LOL!

JJ said...

LOL. Hell, sounds like some of them can give some brothers a lesson or two on "doing whatever it takes to make sure that a woman has her '*ooh wee* moments!" ☺

Glossary

Abbreviations, Colloquialisms, & Vernacular Speech

Please refer below for the meanings of unfamiliar abbreviations and terms used in the essays and conversations.

■ AA—African-American

■ AA—Affirmative Action

■ ABCs—acronym for the "Acting Black Crew"—a subculture of African-Americans who subscribe to a mentality and behavior that runs counter to that of the majority *white* mainstream, i.e. rejecting good school performance, devaluing marriage, etc.

■ Am—Asian man

■ Anywhoo—vernacular for 'anyway'

■ Aw—Asian woman

■ Baby daddy—a man, usually promiscuous, who has children by a woman (sometimes several women) without financial, emotional, and/or legal commitment or contributions, and usually abandons the woman and child(ren).

■ Baby mama—an unmarried woman who has a child(ren) by a man and sometimes several men without securing prior emotional, financial, and/or legal commitment or support

■ B/c—because

■ Bc—black community

■ Bf—black female

■ "BLACK"—a black person who goes to great lengths to demonstrate that they embrace black nationalists views

- Bm—black male/man
- Brotha/brotha(s)/brutha(s)—brother/brothers (usually refers to black men, particularly those in the African Diaspora
- BTW—By the way
- Bw—black woman
- CCBC—central committee of the black community—opinion shapers; those in a black residential area who influence others
- chile—southern colloquialism for 'child'; often used as a term of familiarity or endearment among AAs
- colorism—the belief that lighter/whiter people are more attractive/desirable than darker people
- co-sign—agree
- DBR—damaged beyond repair—refers to a syndrome of undisciplined, irresponsible, destructive, intractable, and sometimes narcissistic, parasitic, violent/deadly behaviors that are usually directed against vulnerable, weaker others
- Diss/dissing—disrespect/disrespecting, insult
- Dog— promiscuous man
- Dunno—'don't know'
- Dyme—a woman considered to be extremely attractive
- Ghetto/ghetto behavior—a pattern of anti-mainstream and often uncouth behavior which includes but is not limited to excessive loudness, inconsiderateness to others, lack of self-discipline, gaudiness, lack of discretion, poor impulse control, disorganized, haphazard and chaotic lifestyle, etc. Poverty may sometimes be a factor in ghetto behavior, but it does not cause it. A ghetto was originally a low-income neighborhood where Jews lived, however in the latter 20th century in the United States, it became a densely populated urban area where

hundreds of thousands of impoverished, disenfranchised American blacks who were victims of systemic racial discrimination often were forced to pay slumlords (99.9% white/Jews) high rents for dilapidated housing. Systemic racial discrimination and the resulting marginalizing and warehousing of millions of African-descended people in inferior housing produced hopelessness in many of them, who came to reject mainstream customs and values. A type of anti-mainstream behavior and lifestyle arose that is now known as "ghetto." In the U.S., many whites, Hispanics, and others also display "ghetto" behavior; however, the term is thought to be most closely associated with low income, urban American blacks.

- "Good" hair—hair with a loose curl or straight, i.e. European textured hair
- Gurl— girl (colloquial term designating affinity)
- Haf mercy!—expression of exasperation
- Ho—whore
- Hoochie–a promiscuous woman
- Hm—Hispanic man
- Hw—Hispanic woman
- IC/ICR—intercultural/intercultural relationship
- IMO, IMHO—In my opinion, in my honest opinion
- IR/IRR—interracial relationship
- Jezebel—persona and stereotype of the temptress/irresistible 'ever-ready' for sex black woman—a stereotype imposed on black females during slavery in the United States to excuse the sexual assaults on black girls and women by white men—for sexual plea-sure and to increase the number of slaves.

- Kinda—kind of
- Lawdy!—an expression of exasperation
- LHM or Lawd haf mercy!—an expression of exasperation
- LOL—laughing out loud, chuckling, mirth
- Mammy—persona and stereotype of a self-sacrificing, self-effacing black woman who neglects her own needs and makes the desires of others a priority; behavior imposed and expected of black women during slavery that is voluntarily still practiced by many AA women.
- 'Nappy' hair—hair with a very tight curl
- Old school—belief in and adherence to customs from an earlier era
- 'On'— arguing, argument, an altercation
- On point—correct, on target
- OMG—Oh My Gosh—an exclamation
- Oow—out of wedlock, not married
- Please!—expression of exasperation, annoyance
- POC—person of color
- PR—public relations
- QLL—quality, loving, and lovable
- Re—regarding
- Sahm—stay at home mom
- Sapphire—persona and stereotype of a loud-mouth 'tough-as-nails' black woman who uses verbal aggressiveness as a means of defense and/or to acquire power or to control others
- Shemale—a woman who thinks it's *normal* to perform the role of a man *and* a woman and willingly performs both roles.
- Sho nuff—sure enough
- Sista/sistah— sister (indicates an affinity with black woman)

- Sista Soldier—a sharp-tongued AA or similar black woman who considers it her prime responsibility to fight all racial slights or other forms of racial inequality, even when her black male peers express apathy and supply no help.
- Smh—shaking my head

- S-o or SO—significant other, steady romantic partner. For ex. a woman's S-o may be her boyfriend, her husband, or a man she dates steadily

- Sorta—sort of

- Stepping up—approaching to ask for a date or to interact romantically with

- trip/tripping/tripping out—verbally combative or aggressive behavior

- U.S.—United States

- VIP—Very Important Person

- Wm—white male/man

- Ww—white woman

- Y'all—you all or you (plural)

Author's Bio & Background of Book

"Evia"— Eve Sharon Moore is an African-American woman, married to a white American man and writes often about interracial and intercultural relationship dynamics. She is the proud mother of two sons, and holds undergraduate and graduate degrees in comparative cultures (ethnology) and counseling. Aside from writing, she devotes herself to appreciating the arts, along with creating and selling her fiber art and jewelry designs. Evia has lived abroad and travels internationally each year.

In 2007, the Associated Press interviewed her extensively regarding her views and the thousands of comments from her readers and spotlighted her site: BlackfemaleInterracialMarriage.com. The site was prominently featured in the AP article regarding the surge in African-American women dating and marrying white men. Her site that began in 2006, soon "morphed" into a popular Ezine that attracted millions of visits. Along with provocative essays and commentary, the site contains numerous photos of black woman-nonblack man couples from all walks of life—from the rich and famous to the ordinary. "With my blog, I wanted to shine the light on the interracial and intercultural marriage options for African-American women. These are other choices that upwardly mobile African-American women have for love and marriage that are not often reflected in the black or white media. I wanted to urge African-American women to take advantage of the many possibilities for love and marriage outside their immediate environment, just as women of other races and ethnicities do."

Evia urges African-American women to "feel free to date and marry any suitable, compatible, loving, and lovable man of quality from any background in the global village. The 'quality' of the man and compatible values are the critical factors—not skin shade," she stresses, and "men of quality come in all skin shades and from all backgrounds. Lots of these guys would love to be given a chance to develop a loving, committed relationship with a black woman."

Each book in the series contains a set of essays, plucked from hundreds of essays she has written, and accompanied by numerous comments from a wide cross-section of international readers. Evia describes herself as "dedicated" to spurring black women towards more fulfilling lives. She implores African-American women to engage in self-love and to promote and protect their interests 'first and foremost.' LIVING WELL: Black Women Interracial and Intercultural Marriage BOOK 4 is the fourth book in the series exploring and documenting black women's views on self-care and the intersection of race, culture, relationships, love, and marriage between African-American women and men from the global village at the turn of the millennium.

ALSO BY EVE SHARON MOORE

1. Black Women: Interracial and Intercultural Marriage Book 1—FIRST AND FOREMOST (Published 2009: for paperback and e-readers)

Essays and Conversations in BOOK 1

~ Nothing Pathological About It
~ A Good Mate Can Be Any Skin Shade
~ Don't Hate Me Because I Married a Good Man
~ The Mating War
~ Why Do People Ask Us How We Met?
~ Black Women—NEVER Accept Scraps!
~ Anger is For Losers
~ The Loving Case—40thAnniversary
~ Do White Men "Step Up" To Black Women?
~ Prison Inmate Lovers
~ Sabotage Again—Do Black Women Push White Men Away?
~ Alec Wek, Black Women's Beauty, and White Men

2. CHOICES: Black Women Interracial and Intercultural Marriage—Book 2
(Published 2009: paperback and e-readers)

Essays and Conversations in BOOK 2

~ Darren and Me—Just 5 Days of Our Love
~ Dating a White Guy?
~ A White Man Responds To 'Dating A White Guy?'
~ Simply Beautiful Love Story!
~ Sisters, Your Life Depends On Your Decisions
~ A Page from History: The 'Little Rock Nine' & Black Women's Standards and   Criteria
~ Associated Press Article Aftermath: Spin—The 'Mules' are Trying to Escape!
~ When He's Not The Marrying Kind
~ Hallelujah! Sisters Are Getting Out Of These Boxes!
~ Thriving While Surviving—The HOT & PAET Approach

3. RECIPROCITY: Black Women Interracial and Intercultural Marriage—BOOK 3 (Published 2010: for paperback and e-readers)

Essays and Conversations in BOOK 3
~ Yes, But Why Did You Marry A White Man?
~ Black Women, White Men, the Mystique–The Real Deal
~ It Pays to Question What You Hear
~ A White Woman's View
~ White Man's Family Rejects Black Wife
~ The Hoax Against Black Women: ONE
~ The Hoax Against Black Women: TWO
~ The Hoax Against Black Women: THREE
~ Me and Him
~ Fear of White Men
~ Colorism and Hair-'ism'—A White Man's View
~ Black Men, White Women—White Men, Black Women

▪ Eve Sharon Moore hopes you enjoyed this book. Please check for upcoming titles of all books in this series!

www.ingramcontent.com/pod-product-compliance
Lightning Source LLC
Chambersburg PA
CBHW022104280326
41933CB00007B/255